MEDITATIONS ON LEADERSHIP

Reflections for leaders of courage and spiritual dedication

LEONARD DOOHAN

Copyright © 2017 by Leonard Doohan

All rights reserved

ISBN 978-0-9910067-9-3

0991006798

The Author

Dr. Leonard Doohan is Professor Emeritus at Gonzaga University, Spokane. He has written 26 books and many articles and has given over 350 workshops throughout the USA, Canada, Europe, Australia, New Zealand, and the Far East. Doohan's recent books include *Spiritual Leadership: the Quest for Integrity* (2007), *Enjoying Retirement: Living Life to the Fullest* (2010), *Courageous Hope: The Call of Leadership* (2011), *The One Thing Necessary: The Transforming Power of Christian Love* (2012), *Spiritual Leadership: How to Become a Great Spiritual Leader—Ten Steps and a Hundred Suggestions* (2014), *Ten Strategies to Nurture Our Spiritual Lives* (2014), and *Rediscovering Jesus' Priorities* (2014). Doohan has also written a series of six books on the theology and spirituality of St. John of the Cross. A further series of books on Scripture, prayer, and the spirituality of laity have recently been re-published by Wipf and Stock. All books are available at amazon.com

For further information, visit leonarddoohan.com

Table of Contents

Introduction 1

Ch 1 Value Leisure as a Component of Leadership 11

    1. Consider the benefits of leisure 13
    2. Enrich leadership with leisure 16
    3. Develop attitudes of leisure 18

Ch 2 Bring Recollection and Focus to Your Life 23

    1. Learn recollection 24
    2. Bring focus to your leadership 27
    3. Train for recollection 30
    4. Facilitate recollection with practical exercises 32

Ch 3 Nourish your Life with Silence 37

    1. Leave noise behind 38
    2. Value silence 40
    3. Seek times of silence 44
    4. Prepare and prolong the effects of silence 46

Ch 4 Appreciate the World in Wonder and Awe 51

    1. Show appreciation 52
    2. Enjoy, discover, and set a new pace of living .. 54
    3. Let the world be your life coach 57
    4. Listen to Pope Francis' challenges 61

Table of Contents, Continued

Ch 5 Identify Your Motivating Convictions 67

1. State your purpose in life. 69
2. Acknowledge what you believe. 71
3. Live with convictions. 74
4. Build your life on ten fundamental convictions 76

Ch 6 Think About Others' Pain and Suffering 83

1. Remember others' pain 84
2. Accept the pain in leadership 88
3. Enter the painful transition of leadership 90
4. Lead in a world of suffering 94

Ch 7 Value People Above All Else 99

1. Understand the consequences of neglecting others 100
2. Lead with graciousness. 104
3. Change focus from self to others 107

Ch 8 Lead with Love 113

1. Be magnanimous 114
2. Show tolerance and compassion 117
3. Transform values with love 120

Endnotes 125

INTRODUCTION

Many people today, and I am one of them, long for a new era when great leaders will rise up among us to serve our communities with genuine concern for everyone. We ardently yearn for men and women who will accept the call to sacrifice themselves for the common good and use their leadership to make a difference to other people's lives. Since we have suffered so long from appalling leadership in politics, business, healthcare, religion, and so on, we appreciate, more than ever, that genuine leadership is special and rarely found. In its finest expression it seems to be only for a prophetical few, for it is a personal calling or vocation. We hope that others will be influenced by authentic leadership when they see it and will share in it at all levels of society—politics, religion, healthcare, business, and so on. This call to leadership that a person senses in the depths of his or her heart sets one apart for a life of service as a visionary who can work with others, inspire and motivate them to implement shared goals for the common good. One cannot train or study for this role even though the acquisition of training, study, and skills will be needed. But this call of leadership comes upon a man or woman as a result of a personal change of heart, an interior transformation that is so strong a person is incapable of refusing the challenge of this call. Such a person knows in the depths of heart and soul that he or she is set apart, life is changed and will only have value in so far as he or she does good for others in building up society. Such leaders are fired with a longing of love for other people's growth and well-being in whatever area of life they find themselves. These great leaders long to be different than the failed leaders of recent decades; they choose a new direction in their lives as they realize their deepest personal needs, hopes, and dreams can only be fulfilled in a life of service to others and to communities.

This calling to leadership can come to anyone in any walk of life or professional commitment, and we hope it does for we need a new kind of leader in business, healthcare, religion, politics, family life, and all aspects of social life. Response to this calling always presumes the acquisition of knowledge and skills—both organizational and interpersonal, but it goes beyond these to bring inspiration, imagination, vision, mutuality, and loving service to everything the leader touches. Leaders today must appreciate what lies beyond the normal horizons of organizational life. They must be able to think, meditate, and contemplate, and they should ask questions that no one else does in the search for what is best for our human communities. Leaders today need to draw out of people a new kind of depth in their commitment to the common good, to unlock the potentials of each one's heart, to create interruptions in the way we have thought about and done things in the past, and especially to motivate people to motivate themselves to achieve what is best for others.

Leaders today must be men and women who are always open to transformation in themselves, others, and organizations. They must be people of collaboration and dialogue in which love, humility, interior freedom, selflessness, and a desire to seek the truth are always part of a commitment to serve the common good and make a difference to other people's lives. These leaders will center all they do on the values of a shared vision pursued with passion and strategic dedication. We need these leaders to have a sense of mystery and awe; to create mutual appreciation and love as distinctive features of organizational life; to encourage creativity in their spirit of service; and to show optimism, enjoyment, and enthusiasm as they develop a hope-filled organization and community.

However, we do not often see this picture of dedication, for our contemporary world is not blessed with many good, dedicated, selfless leaders. Many, if not most, of our contemporary leaders seem hermetically sealed against hope, service of others, and growth together for the common good, and they create an environment of distress and anguish that leaves people feeling lost and without meaning. Instead of visionary leaders with values and dedication, influencing all levels of life with their values, we now have greedy, valueless men and women who buy and support the kind of leaders they want. We have too many old men, and yes mainly men, with tired and irrelevant ideas and images of leadership, and we just cannot get rid of them. Many countries have a leadership class who has ceased to have any useful ideas for the common good. People are so sick and tired of failed leadership they choose idiots as leaders, thinking they will at least shake things up. They pick incompetent and at times violent and immoral individuals just to show the political class how much they hate them. On the other hand, many followers do not want leaders to lead them anywhere. Rather, they insist that their leaders implement their own ideological agendas. In fact, many followers systematically block good leadership, obstructing every initiative for good in order to preserve the status quo over which they have control. These followers do not want to move to an unknown, possibly better future together with others striving for the common good; they want the security of their own—often prejudiced and isolated—past. But little changes! Old leaders in Europe and the Americas clog up society's drains with their corruption, useless approaches to government, lack of change in business practices, the abusive control of healthcare, their irrelevance in religion. We see societies and religions that are incapable of producing leaders who are not dictators. We witness the possessiveness of African leaders, mediocre men who cling to power often with the aid of the military and never give evidence of any leadership abilities. Often the best a country or organization offers is a choice to vote for one or other of two candidates, both of whom are known to be hopeless. Bad leadership is not just in politics; it is everywhere. We all know that systems of government, politics, business, military, education, and healthcare are broken, and while the majority of people and communities want to change them, few leaders rise to do so. Many leaders today are predators and their only motivations are power, money, and status; they are certainly not men or women of humble and generous service. Some leaders in business, healthcare, and the military are out of control in their greed. Trade unions' demands have at times been so excessive they have destroyed their own workers' job opportunities. When many in leadership look at the current national situations they know perfectly well that they are out of control and yet they refuse to fix them. They are attached to the status quo that provides them with opportunities to satiate their greed and corruption. Politicians simply want to win and impose their party's agendas on others with no serious concern for the betterment of society. Religious leaders from whom we have a right to expect more, lack moral stature and allow aberrations of their own religion's teachings or brainwash their followers into believing secondary issues are essential to faith. When we look at the last few decades we see how many innocent people have suffered, lost their financial security, and even died because of the selfishness of their leaders. We can only grieve at humanity's incompetence to solve the leadership problems and needs. Is it too much to expect dedication and service from our leaders? Why are they indifferent to the common good? Certainly, the sun is setting on many leadership styles that may have been effective in the past, and we are so grateful that it is.

Perhaps we have reached a supreme crisis in our ability to find great leaders. Many leaders have a high opinion of themselves but do not receive high grades from their followers who are forced to listen to discussions on the future of society from people who know nothing about it nor care about anything but themselves. One cannot help wondering if we have drifted into a state of semi-consciousness regarding the values that we hope our leaders might have and worrying if we can ever return to a former vitality or whether it is gone forever. When our greatest hope is that our leaders will muddle through their time in office without doing too much damage, we must sadly acknowledge they have no vision and no spiritual depth. We only expect incompetence at best and endless catastrophes at worst. However, when reality and hope are dead, faith is born. When errors of leaders are everywhere and commonplace we must still believe that humanity has within its members a crazy few who will refuse to be beguiled by self-centered corruption to wealth and power, and instead rise up to selflessly serve the common good. Perhaps we can hope for some pockets of leadership in our current sea of mediocrity—a few prophets and visionaries who will lead the people. We need a fundamental change in consciousness for leaders, a reordering of the priorities of leadership that will lead to new life—a few exceptional pilgrims of authentic leadership that can be examples for others in the future. If we do not find this honorable leadership then what is left for us?

What is missing in the lives of our contemporary leaders? Certainly, many who want leadership positions because of the availability of power and wealth lack personal integrity and basic morality and values, and such corrupt people can never lead others to growth. However, there are many men and women in our midst who would willingly serve society with justice and dedication. But, they have few models of good leadership, and at times no idea where to begin to correct current models of leadership and to create alternative visions of genuine service to society. This book offers areas of concentration that will help men and women prepare themselves to better serve and lead and, above all, to become leaders who can make a positive difference to other people's lives. Each chapter of this book gives suggestions for a more fruitful pursuit of values and practices that foster good leadership, and seeks to undermine components of false leadership. If one starts in the wrong direction, moving forward with enthusiasm does not help, it makes things worse. So this book offers components of a healthier approach to life that becomes the foundation for a richer, reassuring leadership that produces the care and management of spiritually relevant values.

1. I would ask those who seek to be good leaders to value leisure in their leadership development, thus undermining the addiction to endless activity so frequently seen in failed leaders. If a leader's life is not healthy, neither will his or her leadership.
2. I urge leaders-in-the-making to bring recollection and focus to their lives, thus blocking the thoughtlessness and scattered responses we so often witness today, unfocused, ad hoc involvement without long term vision for the betterment of society. If a leader cannot find his or her core values, his or her leadership will always lack focus.
3. I ask that individuals nourish their lives with silence and quiet times in which they can think things through, appreciate the impact of their decisions, and learn to listen to the challenges of others and even of transcendent values. The clearest voice a leader must listen to comes in silence.
4. I place before future leaders the challenge to appreciate the world and its people with a sense of mystery, awe, and wonder, so that they can constantly challenge themselves to discover the goodness all around them. For visionary leaders, the world is a teacher, a special guru.
5. I stress the importance for leaders to identify their motivating values, so as to purify the false values and build on the good ones. I call on leaders to tell themselves what they believe in, what for them is the meaning of life, and what is their own purpose in life, since out of this awareness will follow the justness or harmfulness of their decisions.

6. I urge leaders to face the struggles of life, those times of unexpected, breakthrough illumination or painful and purifying periods of darkness. It is important that leaders confront the pain and suffering of others and to view life from their perspective. Spiritual leaders must also accept the pain they will meet in their own leadership. Out of these experiences they must lead in a world of suffering.
7. I plead with those who wish to lead others to treasure people above all else and to treat everyone with graciousness. When so many of our world leaders use and abuse others, it is important that we value all persons in their dignity and potential future growth. Leaders today must treat everyone with respect and reverence.
8. Leaders today cannot lead merely from positions of strength and power since we have seen so often the failures of these approaches. Rather, people need to know that they are loved, and that is the primary task of a leader. Leaders today must have humility and must manage their world with the wisdom of love.

We need a new kind of leader, one who appreciates that leadership comes from within a leader's heart where values and approaches to life are deeply rooted. Such a one will not be led astray by greed, arrogance, and lust for power that we find in so many contemporary leaders. Leaders today must be dedicated to justice, ethical treatment of others, equity, fairness, truthfulness, mutuality, caring, and community building. They must be selflessly committed to changing lives for the better—their own and others'. These are the values that create leaders who make a difference in the lives of people and societies and make up a vision of promise. So, we seek leaders who trust, support, and inspire others; who can freely make choices and decisions in light of a hope-filled future; who have courage and determination to be open to the future and to take risks; who are thrilled at opportunities to empower others, to delegate to them, and to celebrate their successes. This shift in a leader's priorities from self to others comes when one is at peace with oneself and one's own values and approaches to life. Such a leader's calm dedication and determination come from a life built on the convictions and priorities we will discuss in this book and offer to readers for their reflection.

CHAPTER ONE

VALUE LEISURE AS A COMPONENT OF LEADERSHIP

"Leisure is only possible when we are at one with ourselves" (Josef Piper)

People who have been involved in leadership for some time can easily recognize that the best ideas do not come while immersed in stressful work but when one is thinking, reflecting, and at peace. The business of work is often the robber of inner peace. Leaders must create space, time, and attitudes that lead to reflective leadership. Far too many leaders today do not know how to relax. They fill their days with activities that are not always productive, spending disproportionate amounts of time in an office or on their cell phones. They drag out their office time so others think they are hard working. Leisure can bring balance into their days. A little free time can be an opportunity to focus on the values of the spirit and to open oneself to transcendent values through relaxation and creative self-development. A leader can approach leisure as a celebration of life and a rediscovery of perennial values and then commit himself or herself to uproot false attitudes that are contrary to good leadership

One of the most welcoming features of restful leisure is to reestablish control over one's own time. Often overwhelmed by schedules, deadlines, and time restraints, many find liberation in leisure. The question is how to approach the use of this time. It can be an opportunity to enjoy the time to be alone to think, read, meditate, or just relax without interruption. These periods of leisure offer an opportunity to grow mentally and spiritually.

The reality today is that many leaders have more opportunity for leisure than ever in their lives, if they choose to use it. Nevertheless, we do not necessarily see a development of leisure that leads to personal enrichment but often a pursuit of extra work in one's free time to pay for the acquisitions with which our consumer society constantly tempts us. Many people who are now free to develop the leisure dimension of their lives find they do not know how to. They need new values, training, and skills. Those leaders who know how to integrate leisure into their lives are models of wholeness, and many look up to them today, just as previously they admired the models of a work-ethic. Such people who live a leisured approach to life are genuine witnesses to a healthy, balanced life. There are many advantages that result from being enthusiastic about leisure as an essential component of one's leadership responsibilities. It gives more time for reflection, an opportunity to rediscover the values of the spirit, and a chance to foster new friendships. It can open one's mind to new opportunities, help diminish the stress of life and foster healthy living, and lead to a quality presence to others. All these learning experiences have direct effects on one's leadership.

1. Consider the benefits of leisure

Leisure, free-time and relaxation. A correct approach to leisure is a critical component of fruitful leadership. In recent years there are several basic interpretations of genuine leisure, seen either in books or in the way people live out their lives. It is important that leaders confront these components and appropriately apply the right ones to enrich their working lives. The first sees a close relationship between leisure, free time, and relaxation. This approach has good aspects to it but it is not enough. In the past leisure was the prerogative of the rich who did not need to work. Unfortunately, for many, the increase in nonworking hours has led to a fruitless mimicking of a previous leisured class. For many leaders today free time has become a measure of social and economic well-being and can result in empty idleness or be filled with unproductive activities and quantities of so-called leisure goods. For many, leisure is no more than this consumption of nonwork-related goods in their spare time—a sign of status or wealth. In fact, this first interpretation of leisure identifies it simply with the ability to enjoy relaxation. This interpretation, which I suspect is the most common among many leaders today, confuses the real pleasures and advantages of leisure with spending on and enjoying objects of leisure. This confusion about the real meaning of leisure makes many turn leisure into work, thus thwarting the benefits genuine leisure can have on one's leadership. Hence, there have developed many industries around the new leisure needs of society and especially of the working wealthy.

However, this understanding of leisure contains some positive insights, some of which are readily appreciated by people who wish to be good leaders. Some appreciate that there is a close relationship between work and leisure. It claims that the latter can be fully enjoyed only by one who also works— is not necessarily employed, but works. It stresses that there must be a balance between work and leisure for healthy growth. This understanding also affirms that leisure in the widest sense includes ease, rest, and amusement and that it is not merely the idleness and boredom of free time.

The unfortunate aspect of this approach sees leisure either as passivity or injects into free time the same attitudes required in work. There is no real change of attitudes or true rest. Some leaders who are competitive in work are competitive in their leisure, in the acquisition of leisure goods, and in the social image they portray. All this is work and achievement. It is not an integration of work and leisure, but a prolongation of working attitudes into the free time of leisure and it does not enrich the lives of busy leaders as genuine leisure does.

Leisure and creative self-development. A second general understanding, identifiable in recent years, is the equation of leisure with creative self-development. Leisure is not simply freedom from work and obligations. Such leisure can result in boredom, killing time, or filling time. Rather, leisure is freedom for growth, openness to one's inner self and capacities. It is an opportunity to pause and appreciate the wonders of the world around us and grow as human beings in the process. This approach to leisure develops a second well-spring of self-identity outside of one's job that can enrich one's approach to work. It is an occasion to share while free of tension, an opportunity for exercise, fun, and release, a time to stretch interests and revitalize the senses. Leisure is the enjoyment of the natural joys of life and is a time for celebration.

This second understanding of leisure is correct, certainly an improvement on the first understanding, but incomplete. It corrects the negative, passive, and at times stunting elements in the first understanding. In fact, this second one not only refuses to equate leisure and free time but even requires that we give up free time to creative leisure and to genuine recreation. It emphasizes the appreciation that personal development depends on the integration of work and leisure, and that it is the latter which leads to quality growth. Work contributes but only in so far as it is an outpouring of the spirit, in which case it presupposes leisure.

In this view, leisure is the activity in which a leader fulfills the deepest yearnings of his or her heart. The repetition of work does not accomplish this, but the self-discovery and self-development of leisure can. What is learned in the creative effort of leisure can then be integrated into one's approach to the whole of life. Leisure is a happy period because one is privileged to practice those disciplines which enlarge the mind and spirit in the face of the burdens of work. This second understanding, in addition to accepting the need of non-working free time for relaxation, implies a commitment to growth through creative self-expression and indicates the potential value of leisure for the enrichment of the life of a leader. This approach to leisure is particularly important when we see so many of our contemporary leaders as workaholics without depth in their understanding of humanity's needs and hopes, fixated instead on the acquisition of wealth, power, and status.

2. Enrich leadership with leisure

Leisure, leadership, and spirituality. Further reflection suggests a third understanding which stresses a close connection between leisure and spirituality. Leisure is not only free time, relaxation, and creative self-development, it is directly related to total human growth and therefore is intimately linked with enrichment in the leader's life. Leisure is an attitude to life that includes rest and creative self-development, but it also touches the very personal inner spirit of each individual, and each individual must discover it for himself or herself. Finding one's inner self and discovering what renews and reenergizes the inner self is significant on every level of a person's life: human, spiritual, and religious. An approach to leisure that merely brings restful recuperation to complement work, while having no lasting effect on one's inner life and attitudes, is hardly likely to be authentic leisure that can complement one's leadership. Leisure is the relaxation of free time, creative self-development, and a self-tailored approach to life that always enriches all of one's personality and brings enlightenment to one's work and career.

This third understanding presumes that leisure will consist of a broad sweep of values that includes personal, family, social, community, and cultural experiences, all discovered, adapted, and experienced individually. One could suggest all kinds of components of leisure, but it will be up to each leader to decide what is transformative for him or her. Any notion of leisure depends on the understanding we have of the human person, and for a person who is a believer, a humanistic approach to life that excludes the spiritual is not enough to ensure the fruits of leisure. Rather, the total human development that leaders seek must naturally include the spiritual, and leisure is equally necessary at this level. For example, in the appreciative wonder of a restful enjoyment of the universe, the leader is open to values beyond self, to transcendent values, or to the divine. In fact, it is in times of genuine leisure that a person readies self for a conversation about the deepest values of human life. Thus, this third understanding sees leisure as the attitude to life that enables an individual to focus on the truly human, spiritual dimensions of his or her personal integrity and wholeness. For those leaders who have a religious perspective on life, the experience confirms that it is not in the distraction of work but in the relaxed concentration of leisure that one's deepest values explicitly express themselves; leisure is reflection amidst preoccupation. Beyond the affirmation of faith, leisure is equally necessary to experience what we say we believe in; leisure is an intense experience in a cluttered life. Finally, leisure is necessary to nourish the faith we profess and nourishment in a stressful life.

Leisure is also related to what a leader believes. For leaders who are believers dedicated to become spiritual leaders it is important to pause and publicly acknowledge that life is a gift. Do their lives indicate that they believe this? The faith of many, moreover, claims that God graciously gifts people with a wonderful life. Do leaders show they are grateful by enjoying it? People also claim to believe that God is near to us, in us, in others, in the wonders of the world. Only in leisure do they prove this belief by giving time to developing attitudes necessary to meet God. We also believe we can experience God personally and in community, but does our faith show this to others in the life we live? Do we look at everything and see nothing, or do we pause, appreciate, wonder, and praise God who, we believe, reveals the divine self in creation? It is not by work that we gain insight into ultimate values, but in leisure that we appreciate that life is gift. Leisure is the corrective that puts work in perspective and brings forth faith. Genuine leisure culminates in the spiritual. In fact, when it runs its course, it ends in the praise of God. Work never follows that path, unless it is undertaken in a leisurely manner.

A leisured approach to life is a basic element in spiritual growth, for wisdom, and for a focusing on the true values of life. It is not surprising that many leaders rediscover values of the spirit, a profound rediscovery that can even be compared to a conversion. Conversion is not possible without a pause, rest, openness, and for a believer an appreciation of who God is. Leisure offers opportunity for genuine reflection and a quality of wisdom that is closed to hurried, incessantly active, indispensable types. At all stages in spiritual growth, leisure is essentially an attitude to life and hence can be present in very active people at moments of deep involvement. However, periods are necessary when leisure is more intensely lived and expressed; such times of leisure facilitate a leisured approach to involvement in periods of activity.

3. Develop attitudes of leisure

To truly enjoy leisure a leader needs to be content, in other words at peace with himself or herself. A leader needs breadth and balance provided by broad interests, satisfaction in what he or she does, a healthy approach to one's own life, and good support systems, especially friends who provide deep and significant relationships. There are many components of leisure that all leaders can develop.

Rest. Do not be afraid of just sitting down and having a rest. In your regular working life you must show generous dedication to family, social responsibility, the service of others, thinking always of other's needs, but in a moment's relaxation or reflection you can experience something deeper. So do not feel you always have to be doing something, you have earned a rest.

Read. Read something you will enjoy. Books do not need to be related to your career, or planning books, or financial stability, and so on. Rather, read novels, poetry, or light reading. A leisured approach to retirement also offers opportunity to read more about the major issues of politics, world society, philosophy, and religion than regular daily life during employment may offer. Take advantage of this and also of the valuable gift of time for daily reading of something that you find inspirational, possibly poetry, or a philosophy book, or a religious book from your tradition, such as the bible.

Rest and read, but also *relax*. Take a little time each day to make sure you are truly relaxed. If at times you find that you need help in training yourself to relax, then find the help, or follow one of the several sets of exercises that facilitate relaxation. Nowadays, many people cannot relax; they are diseased not because of illness but because they are always worried about something. If you acknowledge a similar need seek professional assistance.

Re-create. Part of every opportunity for a leisured approach to life as an enrichment of leadership is the re-creative component of enjoyable recreation. No one ever grows out of this need. Without falling victim to a consumer approach to recreation, each one can identify an enjoyable pastime that never becomes killing time or wasting time but a pleasant reenergizing new birth.

Rethink. In a time of leisure you can pause, rest, refocus, and rethink some of the values of life that affect your leadership. After rethinking, you may come to the conclusion that the way you previously thought is the way you want to think in the future. You can also think differently. While you have the extra time and are without many of life's pressures, think things over, evaluating your approach to major issues in your life, whether family, social, career, or spirituality and faith.

Rejoice. During the moments of leisurely renewal rejoice in who you are individually, who you are as a member of a family or community. Rejoice in the good things of your life. Rejoice, too, in what opportunities and challenges lie ahead of you and in what the future can be for you. Make your rejoicing practical by trying to bring joy into other people's lives. Remember that work and career is not who you are, it is a component of your life.

Refocus. A break of short leisure is an occasion to examine one's life, to determine what are the really important values of life. By reviewing which aspects of life receive our quality prime time, we can see where the real values of our heart lie. Sometimes we claim things are important to us, but we always assign them secondary time, thus showing us the values in question are nowhere near as important to us as we like to think, or we like others to think. So, examine your life and find out what is truly important to you, what are the quality movements of each day, the significant experiences. During leisure time refocus, prioritize, and determine to give the best of every day to those things that you consider to be the most important in your life.

Renewal is one of the key concepts associated with all leisure. The person who takes time away from regular involvement in work or career can emphasize a single-hearted, single-minded commitment to the renewal of his or her life for self-benefit before anything else, but also for the benefit of a family or of a community. Each one should return from leisure totally renewed. Some people prevent genuine personal renewal by claiming that as soon as they have some extra time they need to work hard on this project or that. Such reactions are sometimes praiseworthy but often are blocks to the restful reflection necessary for a careful directing of one's leadership.

Leisure should be a time of *rejuvenation*. A youthful approach to life gives hope and enthusiasm to others. It is not linked to age. Approaching a period of leisure and re-creative enrichment appropriately, one can develop new attitudes that lead to more integrated lifestyles that show a positive valuing of leisure as well as work. As part of this refocusing, people eager to get the best from leisure should rest, read, relax, recreate, rethink, rejoice, refocus, renew, and rejuvenate themselves.

Developing a leisured approach to complement one's working life can have a significant qualitative impact on one's leadership too. If you can foster a genuine spirit of leisure it will bring added value to all that you do.[1]

Points for reflection and meditation

- *How can leisure improve your leadership?*
- *Specify those things you have learned in leisure.*
- *Think about a time of leisure when you felt renewed.*
- *Which attitudes to leisure are already part of your life and which do you still need to develop?*
- *Why is leisure important to you and your leadership?*

CHAPTER TWO

BRING RECOLLECTION AND FOCUS TO YOUR LIFE

"I close my eyes in order to see" (Paul Gauguin)

Leaders today must be men and women who can think, reflect, reintegrate, and transform the many aspects of their lives. Leadership is no longer based merely on knowledge, competence, and experience, unless these are linked with reflection that produces alternative ways of thinking and acting. In the past we tended to think of leaders as doers and achievers not reflective thinkers. Today's new models of leadership all demand critical reflection, imagination, and an openness to the unknown and the unexpected. The source of real learning in one's leadership is within oneself, and each one must train himself or herself in the new skills needed to be a reflective person. Experience shows that the calmer we are, the more we have access to our creative and intuitive aspects. As we become calmer, we start to see dimensions of a problem we have never seen before.

Without recollection leaders cannot bring forth new ideas, and they lose the opportunity to refocus commitment.

1. Learn recollection

Those leaders who have a mature approach to their leisure time will include in it periods of quiet reflection and recollection. However, a leader should not restrict recollection to times of leisure. In fact, leisure takes extended periods of one's life, whereas recollection is an approach to life and leadership that at first takes a while to develop but later is a reaction that happens in a moment.

There are *two kinds of recollection* that can enrich our lives as leaders. The first is a form of recollection that we can acquire when we use appropriate techniques or practices. The second is a passive experience, an unexpected, focused intuition that happens to us. The second rarely occurs unless we have gained ability in fostering the first, acquired recollection. Recollection refers to the centering or collecting of our thoughts on a particular issue. To achieve this we must block out of our mind all undesirable distractions and collect our thoughts and desires in simple clear attention on issues under consideration. Recollection is not the emptiness one experiences in silence but a refocusing of our thoughts, hopes, or desires on a chosen topic.

Recollection includes an awareness of how thoughts, words, and actions affect our spiritual lives. To be recollected means not being distracted; it means withdrawing attention from some objects in order to give it to others. Recollection requires us to control our senses and faculties. *In calmness we block distractions from our senses* of taste, touch, smell, sight, and hearing, thereby withdrawing from a world of sensations. We must also control distractions from our spiritual faculties of intellect, memory or imagination, and will. We can always gain more information on issues by accumulated input from our senses and faculties and sometimes that can be helpful. However, at times we gain much greater clarity on issues under consideration by blocking the accumulation of information and instead recollecting our thoughts, hopes, and desires, and quietly centering them on a key issue. In this way we become fully present to an idea or thought. In this process we leave aside the discursive accumulation of information and open our minds and hearts to contemplative insight. This is a new way of listening and a new way of knowing. It takes practice and we can often wander or begin to fill our time with additional distracting information, but we should always try to bring ourselves back to recollection.

This process starts with efforts to still our bodies so they do not distract us in times of recollection. These efforts include good posture, stillness, breathing correctly, and healthy diet. No one can reflect meaningfully when he or she is preoccupied, compulsive, hurried, breathing erratically, or suffering the consequences of overeating or overdrinking. So, a simple but important task is to be still, relaxed, with our bodies trained to contribute to the mind's and heart's reflection and recollection.

A further task that prepares us for recollection is *training ourselves in inspiration*. This means giving time to whatever we do, being completely present to people and events, so we can see the inner values and goodness around us. A person prepared to reflect is one who can be inspired by the beauty of nature, by a wonderful piece of music, by artistic brilliance, by children's simplicity, and by others' love, goodness, and dedication. Inspiration means we can discover the inner spirit of events and people. If we can, then we are ready to be inspired by the transcendent in moments of recollection. If we can be inspired by the wonders found in the ordinary, then we will be ready to be inspired by the Spirit.

Another preparatory task to recollection is to *learn to concentrate*. Quick decisions, sound bites, one minute podcast summaries, multitasking, texting, and so on, all have value, but all diminish our ability to concentrate. We live with overviews and superficiality now more than ever. Concentration is an essential component of recollection and prayer. We can train ourselves to concentrate on conversation, on a passage of Scripture, on a piece of music, on a glass of good wine, on a poem, on a child's schoolday events, on a friendship. Concentration helps us see things we otherwise would not, to value people in ways we never imagined, to see the heart of issues that we never used to and, for Christian believers, to concentrate with Christ on the great issues of life.

The further preparatory task to recollection is *the ability to remain in silence,* and we will consider this more in the next chapter. In a world filled so often with noise and distractions, we rarely have opportunity to be quiet, empty, and receptive. We are so full of secondary issues that we cannot recollect our thoughts on central issues or get our fill of the critical values of life. We are blocked by immediate clutter that prevents us from perceiving realities beyond the normal horizons of life. We need to train ourselves to gain distance from the noise, be alone, let nothing happen, sense our emptiness and need, and listen for voices and insights we can never hear without silence. We must train ourselves to cultivate a spirit of watchful waiting for God's interventions in our lives and to silently rest in God.

The second kind of recollection is passive. It is not the result of any immediate effort on our part. Rather, it happens to us—we experience it. This recollection produces an unexpected intuition into the realities of life. It is a wisdom or insight that is greater than that gained by accumulated information or knowledge. It is a new perception that is centered in the innermost depths of our spirit. This passive recollection happens to those leaders who have gained facility in acquiring the first kind of recollection. This one helps a leader solve problems with wordless thought or contemplative insight. Many intricate problems today are not solved by thinking about them but by not thinking about them and letting the mind and heart perceive solutions intuitively and with immediacy. This kind of recollection brings forth new ideas and solutions that are beyond previously accumulated information and knowledge.

2. Bring focus to your leadership

Reflection enables a leader to focus on essentials of life and his or her leadership involvement. Recollection, whether active or passive, leads to a new way of perceiving reality. Instead of accumulating knowledge incrementally, recollection helps a leader refocus his or her mind on essentials with intuitive thought. This redirecting of how one thinks, desires, and acts is a breakthrough experience. It bypasses the ambiguities associated with accumulative information, which may or may not be helpful, accurate, or certain, and in a contemplative moment offers clarity on issues of importance. Leaders in the past needed to master the commonly held knowledge base and the appropriately recognized and accepted skills in order to pursue the desirable goals of organizational life. The understanding and skills of these former knowledge factories of leadership only produce the same results as they did in former years. Recollection is important for leaders for it brings focus and insight not previously envisioned. It produces a new kind of wisdom. Recollection is mysterious, even to the person involved.

All leadership needs focus and *great leadership needs a centeredness* not only in one's thinking but also in one's life. So an important expression of focus for the leader is to hone in on his or her own life; the leader must stop and think with honesty about the core values of life and how they affect leadership. This focusing on self is a remote preparation for the clarity and centeredness that come with recollection. Mature leaders have a healthy self-concept, maintained by an acquired sense of balance. Such leaders recognize their gifts and talents, accept their weaknesses, and nurture their skills for the service of others. Quality leaders are inspirational and have a passion for service. Their commitment is lived with energy, enthusiasm, and excitement. They sense responsibility for themselves, others, and society. Dedicated leaders are reflective and are always learners. They are always asking questions, are open to the spirit, and embody prophetical challenges. So, an important focus for leaders in on themselves and the central values of their commitment to others.

Great leaders who are focused in their dedication *become witnesses to the values they proclaim* and are able to transcend themselves in their selfless service of others. They accept the transforming power of love and, with spiritual perception, seek the more and greater outside of themselves in the community. They are able to see the bigger picture of how their leadership affects life in community. This penetration of unfamiliar depths leads to transformational knowledge beyond conventional categories, a new wisdom that redefines the reality and the response of leadership.

The best leaders are people of inner peace who can integrate recollection into their lives. Leaders are people who offer new horizons to their followers and move people beyond mediocrity and indifference. Such leaders are able to do what they do because their lives are nourished by reflection and prayer. In quiet reflection they discover their true selves, intensify a passion for service, humbly know they must always be open to learn, find their calling in self-transcendence, emphasize the need for balance in life, and move to the growth of a God-given future. This kind of leader finds that recollection nourishes and strengthens his or her life and leadership and brings focus to all that he or she does.

These *leaders are skillful in finding opportunities to reflect and bring focus to their lives*, either spontaneously while out in the country or parks, or by deliberately preparing a part of their home to be conducive to a reflective experience. Much of our contemporary world is distracting and disturbing, but a careful choice of place, artwork, colors, and music can foster the uplifting of spirit needed for genuine reflective prayer and recollection. An experience of recollection cannot be fitted into a tight schedule but needs a prolonged, open-ended time. When many of us are trained to use time well, plan schedules, and use time management planners, it goes against the grain to leave adequate open-ended time for reflection, and yet it is necessary. When we begin to experience emptiness in times of reflection, it often seems appropriate to end, as if we have got the best out of that particular experience. However, the emptiness is frequently what is needed before a new phase with new alternative ideas emerges. Only when one is empty can one be filled with a new reality.

3. Train for recollection

Leaders must *give themselves to deliberate training* for genuine constructive recollection. They must discover practices that are supportive of recollection that thus improve their leadership. This means learning how to collect themselves around a unifying idea and centering on a single issue. Leaders can use several spiritual disciplines to reject distractions and calmly focus and center their thoughts on core values. When leaders' daily lives are bombarded by trivia and constant accumulated images of every kind, a leader who wants to have genuine impact for good in the lives of others must learn how to gain distance from these distractions. The challenge is to live a real life of service in an unreal world of increasing trivia and irrelevance.

However, no one can let into their lives of dedication new spiritual values without first letting other values and ideas out. *A leader cannot cling to old ways* but must let go and be open to a breakthrough experience that comes in recollection. The vast majority of leaders today are clingers, never wanting to let go of approaches to leadership that were considered useful in the past. A new kind of leader must break away from the past and become self-directed in education, training, morality, social involvement, and spirituality.

Part of this self-training for recollection includes renewal in the lives and values of leaders and each one must be willing to become a critical part of this historical change. *Leaders must commit themselves to change.* This requires critical thinking and spiritual courage to stand apart from the superficiality and false values we see in so much ineffective leadership today. This reflective leadership is nourished by recollection that is both soul-searching and soul-stirring and that then enables a leader to focus commitment on serving the common good. Recollection helps a leader enter into the inner space of his or her soul, to appreciate the values of a world beyond the cluttered one of every day, and to see, learn, and value new creative and innovative approaches to thinking about and implementing leadership's vision and values.

Recollection requires stillness, quiet attentive waiting for values beyond ourselves. Growth is a gift, and believers do no more than prepare themselves to receive this gift. However, the attentive waiting is itself an effort that includes many factors that foster an experience of recollection. These persons are comfortable with themselves, at ease with their own strengths and weaknesses, and yearn to identify who they are capable of being. At peace with themselves, they know authenticity is found in the center of oneself; not by having more or doing more but by being more. This inner peace produces creative and visionary leaders. Such people are not afraid to be alone, isolated from others for a while. They do not need to fill every spare moment with activities. They are happy on their own, can enjoy recollection and prayer in solitude, and are aware of the enriching experiences of silence, emptiness, and stillness.

Today we need *leaders with a sense of purpose*, free from distracting and disintegrating secondary values. Their lives are recollected, unified in one great commitment to the vision they pursue for the betterment of others. They are detached from secondary attractions, or rather have integrated all dimensions of life into a single-minded, single-hearted dedication to their purpose in life. Moreover, they appreciate anything that is beautiful: people, senses, music, art, literature, or drama. The ability to experience something beautiful prepares us for seeing the best in others, the best in others' ideas, and for believers, the beautiful experience of God.

4. Facilitate recollection with practical exercises

I would like to suggest eight exercises which are preparatory to reflection and remote preparations for recollection. I also propose that these exercises are preparatory to a more reflective life for a busy leader. As recollection is not possible without them, or something like them, neither is leadership. These exercises have been part of Christianity's ascetical recommendations for centuries. More recently, some of them have also been seen linked to Buddhist meditation in the mindfulness movement. Rather than being restricted to meditation and recollection, mindfulness has come to be understood as a way of being or living in the contemporary world. It is used by some simply to reduce stress by a calm and peaceful acceptance of the fullness of the present moment in which one becomes aware and accepting of one's thoughts, feelings, and surrounding environment. A person achieves this total acceptance by utilizing exercises such as meditation, breathing exercises, concentration on the therapeutic benefits of music.

1. *Listening.* A helpful exercise to prepare for reflection is a self-training in listening, a quality that benefits our leadership. Close your eyes and pretend to be blind, receive all through your ears. Listen carefully for sounds outside the room, then inside the room. Do not hurry this but let it last for five minutes or more. This exercise can help in preparing for recollection, it is also a vital quality for reflective leadership. Really listen to what others say. Block everything else out and just listen. All other qualities added to relationships are wasted if listening is not the first.

2. *Seeing.* For quality reflection, focus on any one point or object. Any training like this is a training for recollection and concentration on the decisions we encounter in leadership. When you look at a thing it changes you. Pay attention to the ordinary until you see what is of value. This prepares for the faith encounter of recollection; it takes time and restfulness. This seeing beyond the immediate picture helps leaders get away from the tyranny of petty laws and the way things have always been done and to see something else. This self-training in listening also helps the leader to see and read a situation accurately.

3. *Sitting Still and Doing Nothing.* Leaders who wish to commit themselves to recollection know the importance of the body for quality reflection and prayer. They take diet and exercise seriously and appreciate that the Christian tradition of fasting can have a healthy impact on a life that is reflective. With

experience, each person finds an appropriate and comfortable posture, a position they can stay in for the prolonged period of reflection on values, ethics, mission and so on. This approach needs nourishing with ongoing education in values, complemented with good literature of all kinds and an awareness of contemporary world events. It is difficult to give quality leadership to others without ongoing education.

4. *Relaxation*. Relax. A vital quality for recollection, this is also vital for a healthy leadership. We need to resist the competitive consumer-society in which we live. We do not always have to show power, drive, or insight. We do not always need to share, contribute, dialogue, discuss. So much spirituality is permeated with compulsiveness. However, some of the greatest Christian qualities will always be important-abandonment, passive commitment to God, openness to divine providence. Relaxation fosters inner peace and thus opposes the robbers of inner peace—frustration, fear, worry, anxiety, conflict, guilt, and ineffective adjustment strategies.

5. *Development of the Other Senses of Taste, Smell and Touch.* We all have touch hunger and anxiety. We all need to touch and to be touched. This surfaces also in our intense desire to be in contact with others and to share values with those around us. It surfaces in the need to have close personal relationships with the others who are significant in our life. We also develop focus with our senses in the enjoyment of music and the intensification of objects of our other senses of smell and taste.

6. *Worship by Affirmation*. This and the next, are great aids to recollection and reflective leadership and help us develop benevolent attitudes in our leading of others. Look at a scene with concentration and from it raise your mind to ultimate

values and to God its maker. See anything in the scene of positive value, admire this, and affirm it to perfection. This training to focus on the positive has lots of practical consequences in leadership such as approaches to performance appraisal.

7. *Worship by Detachment.* As above, look and concentrate, but this time find what is not of ultimate worth and admire its opposite. Affirm the opposite and ask for the purification of the negative human quality. In this you should not become involved in the human negative, but immersed in the positive that is attainable. It helps us maintain distance from the negative we find in our organizational work. This practice can counteract the tendency among many leaders of selective perception—seeing only what they want to see.

8. *Breathing Exercises.* This is a training in calmness for prayer and life. While developing calmness, it deepens our awareness of the care of the Lord for us, and our dependence on the Lord. The contemplative exercise and the conviction on ultimate values of life and love go together. This exercise, complemented with the use of a mantra, focuses our thoughts and reflection.

We have reflected on the links between recollection and leadership. What prepares us for the former can profoundly influence the latter. A great leader creates a sense of the spiritual within himself or herself as well as within the organization. Most organizations today do not need plans and strategies, they need a healthy spirit that is life-appreciating and life-giving. For the spiritual leader leadership is not an occupation but a deliberate choice that permeates all life, physical, intellectual, emotional, and spiritual. We can best achieve the results of these exercises by carefully choosing appropriate space and time so that they readily facilitate recollection, focus and peace of mind and heart. This choice of our own sacred space and sacred time can enrich each day, our leadership style, and our entire lives.

Points for reflection and meditation

- Do you include in each day times to think, reflect, and reintegrate the events of the day?
- How do you make stillness, inspiration, concentration, and silence intimate components of your leadership?
- What brings a sense of centeredness to your life?
- Do you look forward or backward, do you cling to secure ideas from the past or are you always ready for change?
- What exercises do you do daily to facilitate recollection?

CHAPTER THREE

NOURISH YOUR LIFE WITH SILENCE

"Silence is a source of great strength" (Lao Tzu)

When a leader can discover the enriching aspects of genuine leisure and learn how to cultivate a spirituality that includes recollection, then such a leader can be ready to move on to including periods of fruitful silence in his or her daily life. When a leader can leave noise behind, value silence, and deliberately train himself or herself to seek times of silence, then such a leader can develop an ability to listen to the sounds of silence at any time during the day. So, he or she prolongs silence and its healthy effects throughout the day. No matter what this kind of leader is involved in, he or she can enter silence and bring its benefits to whatever task is at hand. Part of such a leader's awareness is always centered within his or her inner spirit, even when the rest of one's consciousness is focused on the immediate task.

This leader automatically responds to any problem by moving beyond recollection and by withdrawing into silence and intense listening, even though others may never appreciate he or she is doing so. Silence enables this leader to become a deep listener who in silence can discover multiple perspectives to an issue, discern options and possible responses, and value the gifts and potentials of co-workers. A leader who values silence is a person of wisdom who can find harmony, enlightenment, and peace amidst the burdens of daily life.

1. Leave noise behind

Beyond leisure and the enrichment and joy it brings to intensely dedicated lives, and beyond one's self-training and passive reception of the centeredness and focus that comes with recollection, there lies silence. A gifted leader who wishes to give himself or herself to improving other people's lives will courageously enter the seeming emptiness and helplessness of silence. There, in total passivity, one is alone and in that solitude confronts oneself in simplicity and rawness otherwise rarely experienced. *This encounter with silence is a source of great strength.*

It is not easy to enter silence. Today, all of us, leaders included, live in an extremely noisy world. There is rarely in a day an opportunity for a little quiet time away from computers, phones, social media, and other people's constant demands. Life and leadership are beautiful mysteries but we hardly ever have the peace and quiet to appreciate them in an increasingly noisy world. Thoreau in "Walden" accurately described contemporary life when he said, "our life is frittered away by detail." It is true that our days are filled with mind-numbing and spirit-numbing activities along with daily leadership practices and responsibilities.

Leaders are burdened by these activities and responsibilities, overwhelmed by a pattern of thoughtless communications that sweeps over them every day. *There is no time for silence.* The amount of daily "stuff" a leader must consider slows down genuine needed decisions, blocks new ideas, and leads to an intellectual laziness that stunts creative development. A day without some quiet time to gather and prioritize one's thoughts can erode one's spiritual vision and commitment. At times we silence our own inner spirit and diminish our ability to discern and discover what is best for ourselves and our service of others. We must resist the pressures of contemporary artificiality and trivia and spend our time on things that matter and on decisions that make a difference to other people's lives—and these we discover in silence.

It takes a child about two years to learn how to speak, but *it can take a lifetime to learn how to value silence* and be willing to embrace it. Instead, leaders listen to the bombardment of words every day on television, robo calls on the phone, politicians who cannot shut up, and commercials that treat everyone like idiots. Unfortunately, many leaders have no ability to listen to silence. When they witness silence it is often the result of suppression, subjugation, a form of punishment, a means to disempower others. Today's society values speech more than silence. But speech can discourage thought as we see in politics, it can hide what is not said as in business practice and commercials, it can protect others from irresponsibility as sometimes in healthcare, and it can cover up ignorance as often happens in religions. It can also be an escape from one's inner self. We are in a period of history when we say "talk is cheap," when we refer to many in leadership positions as "talking heads," and when we increasingly witness many leaders who think they have all the answers before they have ever listened to the problems. We have leaders who hire experts to talk for them, others who can talk their way out of any problem, and many who are daily given "talking points." Talk, talk, and talk. Leaders today frequently talk endlessly to avoid communication and few if any seem to value silence. But to be a great leader one must leave noise behind.

2. Value silence

If we welcome silence, silence will welcome us. Silence is a wonderful response when we have nothing to say. Those who love us understand our silence. Often those who do not love or know us cannot understand our words when they cannot understand our silence. *Silence is often the best response* to the wonder of friendship, of love, of the beauty of the world. Silence between friends speaks volumes. Words are valuable up to a point and then silence takes over. Silence is often a sign of great strength and inner security. When we nurture our lives with leisure and punctuate them with recollection we may be ready to enter silence. Sometimes we need to be alone; for it is in silence we learn true wisdom.

Beyond these momentary responses of silence there is *the spiritual discipline of silence*, practiced by dedicated people for centuries; a discipline that can also enrich our lives and leadership. As with the practice of recollection, we begin by calming our bodies and minds and letting go of all distracting thoughts, hopes, desires, and bodily reactions. We must surrender ourselves to tranquility, quietness, and solitude. We must find the emptiness that leads to receptivity. So, entering silence is first an acquired discipline. Unlike the times of recollection when we seek to focus our entire selves on a single issue, in silence we seek to empty our minds of all thoughts, our imagination of all hopes, our will of all desires, and our bodies of all movements, deliberate and spontaneous. So, we control all our senses and faculties, both natural and spiritual of all the usual distractions that we deal with each day. These distractions are the immediately obvious ones, but once we control them there arise other soft, background noises we do not normally hear, even though they are always there. We cannot exist in a soundless world. In fact, it can often be helpful in maintaining silence to play some non-distracting music. This drowns out the secondary noises just as the repetitive use of a mantra does. Above all silence refers to inner stillness, the spiritual discipline that enables one to touch one's inner self.

When we speak of silence we refer to times and experiences when there are no sounds, no verbal communication; a time when everyone refuses to speak. It can be energizing if we give sufficient time and resist the temptation to fill the emptiness with noisy words and thoughts. Unlike recollection which is a focusing on a particular thought or issue, silence is a time in which we go *beyond recollection to empty ourselves of all issues*. In this silence one comes face to face with ultimate values of the spirit. These will include awareness of oneself and one's role in the world, the importance of other people in our lives, the beauty of the world around us, and appreciation of a realm of life beyond this one. These components of true vision come in silence and give meaning to our lives. Silence is the time when we see our true selves, when we touch a different part of our hearts and minds, a different level of our humanity. In silence our minds and hearts work through issues on their own, wordlessly and thoughtlessly. We do not think about them; we experience them. We do not concentrate or focus on an issue as in recollection. Rather, we passively experience a new way of appreciating values.

In quiet times we *discover a freedom from negative emotions* and thoughts, gain a capacity to perceive clearly and control our own thoughts and decisions, and live in the here and now. In silence a leader can enter a deeper level of understanding and in the experience discover new possibilities for solutions, planning, and organizational life without thinking about them. Such a leader can then become a pioneer or a prophet of a new vision. In silence we can, as it were, stand back and observe ourselves and see whether we like what we see. Silence is not complete passivity, nor total emptiness; in fact we can hear voices in silence that we never hear at any other time. In silence we can learn more about ourselves, we can see solutions that otherwise never occur to us, we can appreciate values that we miss in a cluttered life. Silence is the context for learning to listen and to discern; it is an opportunity for transformation. These skills enable one to become a leader of the future.

We must *value silence and enter its times with respect and reverence*. It is a period devoid of noise but never just empty. It is an occasion for gentle, spiritual presence and listening. A time of emptiness, yes, but an experience of emptiness that is pregnant with a new listening that leads to subtle inspiration and guidance. Emptiness is not weakness but strength. We stop thinking, celebrate quiet times, leave aside inadequate words, still our thoughts, calm our emotions, and listen intently. Emptiness results from total control of distractions, leads to peace, and brings the silence that helps us prepare for receptivity. Leaders who are full of themselves have little to offer others; those who appreciate emptiness can make a difference to others' lives.

Silence can be wordless communication, a new way to listen and to hear. We should never underestimate silence, for it can be productive—a silence that nourishes a busy life. It creates *an opportunity to experience the well-spring of values* that we have treasured and to remember traditions that have nourished our lives. Silence is the corrective to our world's excessive talking. We need silence to achieve inner stillness, to prepare for transformation, and to think about the importance of life's critical events. In silence a leader can gain knowledge and insight to help determine what is best for others.

This commitment to silence requires courage to accept our own human ability to *go beyond the limitations of mind and heart* that many men and women impose on themselves. We can experience a vitality that transcends the ordinary and participates in a level of life that is self-affirming and reaches out beyond our present world to another realm of life that gives meaning to our present one. A person can emerge from silence aware of a transcendent presence that gives meaning to everything one does. One can emerge from silence aware that there is more to life than just the narrow superficial understandings and responses common in leadership today. Silence gives one the ability to capitalize on the spiritual force deep within one's heart and a great leader then pursues the dream with enthusiasm and excitement.

3. Seek times of silence

A spiritual leader hungers for silence, aware that it is the best opportunity to access his or her creative and intuitive self. In the calmness of silence leaders gain contemplative insight into problems and life direction and see aspects of responses they never see at other times. Sometimes this experience just happens to us and we welcome it into our hearts. For example, at times we see problems or critical issues in our world and the only possible reaction is silence. We can be shocked into silence by the prejudice, violence, or hatred in our world—aware that words cannot explain what we witness. We can also be immersed in silence by the revelation of goodness and beauty we see—aware that it tells us something about the mystery of who we are called to be as human beings. Beyond these moments when we are thrust into silence, there has to be a commitment to the deliberate pursuit of silence.

Leaders must *create a sacred space of silence and a sacred time of quiet*. This is where men and women can grow as leaders. Many commentators say you only learn leadership through experiences. That is not true. Leadership is learned by experiences critically assessed in silent times when one's own mind wordlessly evaluates and guides future decisions and actions. After all, leaders do not get their best ideas when involved in the intensity of distracting work. Rather, they get their best ideas in times of quiet reflection, and beyond these reflective times there are periods of silence and solitude that nurture them without them being aware of them. Moreover, they should not fill quiet times with lots of thoughts, but rather allow their minds to work on their own in silence and then to discover answers intuitively. This happens in periods of seclusion, silence, and personal crisis (crisis is a Greek word meaning times of new judgments). A skilled leader will insert himself or herself into this process that leads to personal transformation.

Spiritual leaders must seek enriching passivity in a world of action, and sometimes of useless activity. Leaders must *set aside quiet time each day to empty their minds* of distracting noise and remain receptive without filling their minds with discursive words or thoughts. This gives them occasion to see reality no longer in parts and pieces but with a revelationary, contemplative glance that reshapes our perception of reality. Silence is not always productive, but at times it enables us to see in a moment's intuition the whole picture. Many leaders with cluttered minds see things immaturely in parts—some parts dominating at one time and others at another time. When some aspects dominate, others deteriorate and even fade away and are lost. Silence can enable mature integrated vision of issues. In such silence a leader finds greater meaning in issues under consideration, interprets them according to a higher order, and discovers inspiration and understanding that can empower others.

In the silent times they set aside each day leaders must detach themselves from all the sophisticated techniques that the leadership industry has built up over the years and trust their inner spirit to discern what leadership's methodologies and programmed responses fail to attain. Leaders *must trust the spiritual path of silence*, recognizing that deep within their inner spirit and soul there is a zone where they find their true selves and see and hear more perceptively than they ever do when drowning in contemporary leadership's analyses and programmed responses. The insight that leaders mature from the inside out and not from the outside in changes the way we approach both leadership and life. Likewise spiritual leaders see the invisible as more important than the visible and the spiritual than the material. These self-defining choices are discovered in silence.

4. Prepare and prolong the effects of silence

A reflective and contemplative leader cherishes times of withdrawal in silence and seeks to manifest a series of attitudes that maintain and guarantee his or her approach to silence. A leader who nurtures these attitudes to life constantly prepares for silence and with the same attitudes prolongs its effects.

1. Nurture values of the Spirit. A leader can prepare himself or herself for silence by nurturing the values of the Spirit. One nurtures the values of the Spirit in reflection, inspirational reading, shared discussions with like-minded leaders, and prayer. This requires an openness of heart, an appreciation of beauty, a liberty of spirit, and a dedication to goodness. Such a leader not only leads well, he or she also lives well—a model of leadership's best values, a model of the best values of humanity. So, he or she creates opportunities for reflection and recollection, gives quality time to others in genuine friendship, reads material that uplifts the spirit, and patiently and kindly brings healing to any hurts in the organization.

2. Listen to the gentle reminders of the Spirit. If leaders are to benefit from silence they must be great listeners, not only to formal and informal input of others, but also to what motivates, inspires, and satisfies others. A leader must listen to others' felt needs, imagination, and dreams, especially when they refer to change or alternative ways of seeing things. A great listener listens to self, others, organizations, industry developments, and markets, but also to the signs of the times, the hopes of humanity, the yearnings of the needy, and the world's cries for help. Sometimes one can listen to and learn from the loud voices of our world. On other occasions one can listen to the gentle word of the Spirit in others' frustrations, in people's reactions to failed decisions and practices, in followers' rejoicing in organizational successes, in the hopes of the discriminated and oppressed, in the stories and cries of those who suffer. A great leader learns to listen to voices from wherever they come.

3. *Be open and receptive to what life brings.* A gifted leader knows the best qualities of life are those he or she has received, and consequently appreciates the need to be open and receptive to what life brings. This prepares a leader to also be receptive in times of silence. There is an ongoing youthfulness about such a leader, an excitement regarding what could happen next, and a constant openness to hope. Drive and determination give way to reflective time, a quieting of one's spirit, a restful aloneness that readies one to receive, and an awareness of one's emptiness and need. Some contemporary leaders in all forms of organizational life are so full of themselves, so confident of the little they know, so certain of their grasp of the vision, so messianic in the roles they assume, that they are incapable of learning and are destined to be ignorant and incompetent for life. Reflective leaders are open and receptive to God, others, the environment, social trends, and the cries of humanity.

4. *Be grateful for the gifts of life.* Leaders should have a positive mental attitude and a healthy self-esteem. With these attitudes he or she enters a silence that can be productive. They know their gifts, appreciate them, and can thus expect more of themselves. Gratitude is a special quality of a thoughtful leader. He or she is enthused about the community's many gifts and becomes a focal point of expressions of gratitude to all. Colleagues and followers know the leader appreciates them, and they give more of themselves, knowing the leader will receive their dedication with gratitude. The leader will create opportunities to celebrate the successes of others, either informally while passing someone in the corridor, or more formally in community celebrations.

5. *Discern the presence of goodness.* Training for the practicalities of discernment help a leader in the intuitive discernment that can come in silence. The leader must choose freely from alternatives, selecting what is the best and leaving aside what is not. This will include flexibility, creativity, imagination, and innovation to reframe issues to discover the best. While organizations often dislike change, the leader must encourage followers to question, challenge, analyze alternatives, and be courageous enough to change. This leader trains followers for healthy skepticism, constructive criticism, and forceful hope. There is goodness in every aspect of life. Negative developments can have good side-effects; obstacles we encounter have potentialities for good. In a world that stresses negativity, a reflective leader who has experienced the goodness of God's gifts focuses on goodness wherever it can be found.

6. *Be humble in all you do.* The enrichment of silence is a humbling experience. The reflective leader is a leader of hope.

Such a leader will need determination, perseverance in efforts, and courage to plow ahead to new goals. This sense of confidence will need to be balanced with humility, for people have given up on arrogant, overbearing leaders. Today's leader lives with uncertainty, knows he or she no longer has all the answers, is ready to accept new ways of doing things, and appreciates the best ideas can come from anywhere in the organization. Aware that everyone has gifts of one kind or another, he or she gives people confidence to act on their own authority. For a leader who is humble, silence is always productive.

7. Cherish others and their gifts. The leader has to really care about other people, help them continually through example, and have a passion for their success. When followers know they are trusted and admired, they are motivated to do more in giving their discretionary commitment and thus exceed what was expected of them. As part of valuing other people and their contributions, a leader will strive for inner integrity to be the genuine person his or her followers deserve. He or she will model the values for which others should strive, set an example that others can emulate, and treat everyone with respect, dignity, and justice. The leader who cherishes others will create a climate of mutual trust, will coach and guide them, influence them to be visionaries, foster their self-leadership, and inspire the commitment to the community's shared vision. Such a leader enters silence ready to be enriched in his or her inner life and values and to discover and cherish the giftedness of others.

8. Be a gift to others. A good leader influences others to exceed themselves. He or she gives followers a sense of their own maturity and wisdom in leadership. The leader can give others the opportunities to utilize their gifts. Delegation, collaboration, shared mission values, subsidiarity, empowering individuals and teams, are all ways to give others the space and occasions to grow and appreciate their own gifts. Being a gift to others also means being a good leader. More than anything else, the leader is a gift to others in showing love and encouragement. Always more effective than adversarial roles, love builds up others and gives meaning to their lives. His or her whole life is to be modeled on self-gift in loving service to others. In silence he or she appreciates that selfless love of others makes sense.

These approaches to daily life help us welcome silence as a friend and make it part of our growth as leaders. To understand silence one has to be mature in other aspects of one's life. Giving oneself to times of withdrawal in silence takes more maturity than the seeking of genuine leisure or cultivating of authentic recollection.

Points for reflection and meditation

- *What do you do to bring quiet into a noisy world?*
- *Specify what you believe could be the positive contributions of silence to your life.*
- *Do you have a special space and time to center yourself in silence?*
- *What do you do to nurture the values of silence?*
- *How do you see yourself as a gift to others?*

CHAPTER FOUR

APPRECIATE THE WORLD IN WONDER AND AWE

"The most beautiful things in the world must be felt with the heart" (Helen Keller)

A leader who can discover the benefits of genuine leisure, recollection, and silence not only becomes more reflective and contemplative but also becomes more sensitive in all aspects of life—self-assessment, relationships, perceptive analysis, and values-oriented planning. These and other qualities make a leader more attentive to others and to organizational developments and especially to the values, inherent goodness, and giftedness that are readily seen throughout society. Appreciation is an exceptional quality in a spiritual leader. Of course, it can be artificially used by anyone as a leadership technique, but genuine appreciation comes from the heart of a leader, and followers can always distinguish between heart and technique. In this chapter we look at a leader's ability to appreciate the beauty of the world, both static in nature and dynamic in organizations. These perceptions and value decisions become part of a leader's approach to people and organizations. They help form a leader who can make a difference to other people's lives.

1. Show appreciation

The gift of leadership includes vision; it means seeing what other people do not see and looking at issues in ways other people do not. This is important because leadership takes creativity and imagination. Leaders must be skilled in looking beyond the ordinary, obvious, and visible to discern responses that non-leaders never see. So, *a key quality for leaders is a sense of appreciation* whereby they can perceive what others do not. We hear suggestions that leaders should utilize appreciation days, use words of appreciation, or write letters of appreciation, but the quality and skill—even gift—of appreciation that we consider here goes beyond these simple gestures. When a leader appreciates something or someone, it means he or she shows regard or respect, offers a favorable judgment, shows understanding of the worth and value of someone or something. This special leadership quality of appreciation includes perceptive discrimination or discernment as when one sees and truly understands the good qualities or full growth potential of someone or something. We sometimes use the word "appreciation" to refer to the recognition and enjoyment of something or someone. Or, again, we see the word used to express gratitude, admiration, or approval of people or events. Yet again, appreciation can refer to a sensitive understanding of a work of art or a gifted person. These commonly used expressions of this special word "appreciation" form a synopsis of what an exceptional leader does. He or she appreciates people and their gifts, appreciates the pros and cons of situations, and appreciates his or her own calling and its mission. Of course, we also say that something appreciates in value, and that is certainly the case with any organization that has leaders who know the value of everyone with whom they work and can appreciate each one in depth.

One of the many problems of the failed leadership we see all around us is that *many contemporary leaders are insensitive to other people,* fail to value their gifts, and do not understand their pain and suffering. They seem ignorant of world events, are narrow minded in their approach to life, and legalistic and fundamentalist in their pursuit of values. They lack the gift of appreciation and seem unaware of how effective and powerful appreciation can be. Books on leadership extol appreciation of workers as a way to inspire, motivate, and encourage them in their commitment. Furthermore, appreciation of events and issues leads to greater understanding and thereby success in one's leadership. Appreciation leads to depth of understanding in what one does but it also leads to greater maturity in the leader.

Appreciation includes attentiveness when a leader is observant, thoughtful, and perceptive towards others and events. Attentiveness in a leader means paying close attention to someone or something and includes the concentration and focus we considered in earlier chapters on recollection and silence. But, attentiveness also implies a diligent consideration of others, thoughtfulness towards them, and a willingness to take care of others' needs with courtesy. Appreciation includes attentiveness, and attentiveness leads to deeper appreciation. This interrelationship of these two beautiful leadership qualities moves a leader to a further quality, namely a sense of wonder. The more one is attentive and appreciative the more one becomes surprised at the exceptional one finds in people, events, communities, and organizations.

It is delightful when *a leader is able to admire the exceptional in others* or in situations, to be amazed at the gifts, beauty, value, and goodness he or she sees all around. Wonder also includes a sense of curiosity and even a little doubt and uncertainty as one raises questions about the true nature of events or people's reactions. This kind of reaction leads to a special kind of appreciation and wonder, namely "awe" which goes beyond wonder to add reverence and even fear to one's reactions. Awe in a leader is an overwhelming feeling of admiration and reverential respect. These qualities of leadership cannot grow without the foundations of leisure, recollection, and silence.

2. Enjoy, discover, and set a new pace of living

Appreciation of the world around us in wonder and awe emerges from times of leisure, recollection, and silence. It can be *nurtured by joy, a sense of discovery, and a new pace of living*. Leaders can look at joy in one of four ways. First, they can find joy in personal pleasure and gratification. Such leaders, and there are many of them, focus exclusively on themselves and have no interest in anyone else or the common good. A second group of leaders finds joy in personal achievement in their work. They compare themselves to others, always wanting to be better and more successful than those around them. A third group is made up of leaders who see themselves as involved in something bigger than themselves and find joy and happiness in making a difference in other people's lives. They appreciate that other people's lives matter to them, and they impact very positively all those around them. The fourth group is made up of those leaders who appreciate a realm of life beyond this one and who find joy in unconditionally giving themselves to transcendent values, and with wisdom they pursue truth, fairness, justice, and unconditional love towards everyone. In this pursuit they find a desire to give themselves to the call and challenge they feel to serve others for the greater good. In this appreciation of others they find a thrill and joy.[2] Leaders who value appreciation can savor life and the people and events of each day, and because they appreciate others, they can rejoice in their achievements. This joy is a delightful aspect of leadership, a chance to be present to life in a new way; fully present to savor both the joy and the pain. Such leaders have time to be with people in compassion and love, to sympathize and to empathize with them. They do not need to rush from one event to the next, from one person's presence to another's. They enjoy being with people and valuing their gifts and talents.

Appreciating others includes the spirit of discovery towards people, events, and responsibilities that are part of one's life, finding qualities and talents even they were unaware of. It can lead to a willingness to take more risks than ever before, to reinvent themselves, to do unimaginable things in making a difference to other people's lives. Discovery means leaving something behind to search for something new. It may be a deeper insight, a refinement, or a broadening of skills, a new way of doing something, a new contribution to vision from followers, or something entirely different. The approaches necessary to discovery are the ones that emerge from a sense of appreciation and make leadership fulfilling and exciting. This comes to leaders through reflection and a refocusing on life's meaning, on one's role and destiny in this world, and on one's mission in serving others. Leaders who have the gift of appreciation can see connections they have never before understood. With time, reflection, and a new vision of life, such leaders discover new aspects of their relationship to others that give greater meaning to life.

Mature leadership *requires of us a new approach to daily living*. We have seen that it includes leisure, recollection, and silence, but it also includes a different pace of living. Nowadays, in some parts of the world there is a movement that speaks of "slow living," "slow cities," and "slow meals." The people dedicated to this movement seem to reject those aspects of modern experience that expect us to rush everywhere, pursuing the fast life in the fast lane, stopping only for fast food. But some people today value an approach in which they slow down, enjoy life, savor food and friendships, and truly appreciate their role in the world. They try to give quality time to everyone they meet and to everything they do. Living slowly means each one should go slow, be quiet, take time, and think about the quality of his or her life. "Slowness" is modern, and you will find it very quickly in cities all over Europe. There you can slow down and enjoy the time you have rediscovered in a new approach to leadership. "Slowness" is a movement, a network of hundreds of cities in ten countries all dedicated to the beneficial slow rhythms of life and to plans for well-being.

"Slowness" is a deliberate decision against the fast life, against the useless rushing around that gets confused with efficiency, against situations in which the rhythms of machines take precedence over the rhythms of people. It is a precise decision to oppose those styles of life that lead to the extinction of what is truly human. Contemporary leaders can now include in their daily lives words such as "slowlife," "slowfood," "slowfit," "slowsmoke," "slowbook," and "slowcity." People dedicated to this movement live well, live in appreciation of the environment, live in careful attention to the rhythms of their own bodies, live with a love for art and culture, live amidst architecture that fosters beauty and the uplifting of the spirit. People dedicated to "slowness" *seek to become connoisseurs of life.* Their's is a special kind of appreciation of life from which we can all learn.[3]

3. Let the world be your life coach

When leaders appreciate the world in wonder and awe, the *world can then become a special guru* for them, a life coach that can teach them many lessons about life and leadership. When a leader has learned to relax in genuine leisure, trained himself or herself in recollection, and discovered the value of silence, he or she appreciates and perceives levels of life in people and organizations of which others are never aware. First, leaders see that the world and its values have an alluring aspect that spiritual leaders must renounce. Some who do not have the gifts of reflection of which we have spoken can be tempted by the urge to possess and control the world around them—its people and its organizations. Thus, we see so many corrupt leaders who waste the earth and its peoples. Second, once leaders are able to appreciate the world of people and organizations as presenting at times temptations to their integrity, they can move beyond this negative assessment to see that they can use the world in all its aspects to serve the common good. They can appreciate how the use of this world's goods and an ability to channel gifted people and institutions can lead to the service of others and the betterment of society. A third approach to the world by reflective and appreciative leaders is that it offers people the opportunity to appreciate its harmony, beauty, bounty, generosity, and wonder.

A spiritual leader sees that there can be a better world of business, politics, culture, and social life. All form part of the dynamic fabric of our world, and a spiritual leader appreciates that all these aspects of organizational life can be drawn away from misuse, healed, and redirected to serve the common good. Each can have its own beauty and excellence. A spiritual leader understands that *human organizations have their own beauty* and can be channeled to work in harmony and peace.

A reflective leader can also appreciate the awesomeness of architectural achievements, the successes of political efforts for peace and the common good, the beauty of loving relationships, and the generous self-sacrifice of volunteers. *Great leaders find so much they can learn from the world.* Some people look but never see; great leaders are attentive to all around them in creation and in the human community, and they are inspired, motivated to contribute to the common good, enlightened in their service of others, and discover renewed dedication in their leadership. When greedy and corrupt leaders amass their fortunes and travel the world, they do not appreciate the world; their joy is in amassing, in having all this stuff, and in doing what others cannot. A leader who appreciates the world in wonder and awe treats the people with whom he or she works differently and accepts the potential of organizations to achieve great things for others. Such a leader sees people's gifts and goodness and knows organizations can work efficiently and be part of a better human community.

When a leader dedicates himself or herself to work within the dynamic organizations of society, he or she learns that they can serve the common good and that they can only be misdirected or abused by greedy, selfish human beings. A leader learns how the best results come when all parts work together, interdependently, each part contributing to the progress of the whole. *Everything works best when all work together.* The leader also learns the values of change, that creativity, and adaptation can give new life to organizations and that prudent watchfulness is needed to avoid misuse. Working with organizations teaches leaders a lot about their own leadership.

The natural world in which we live and move and exist is a special source of inspiration and guidance for all human beings. Spiritual people of every generation, including our own, see *natural creation as revealing the mysteries of God* and challenging men and women to imitate its goodness, beauty, and generosity. In creation we see the wonder of the Creator and many spiritual people find that the beauty of the world reveals the beauty of God, and its natural laws, interrelationships, never-ending generosity, total service of humankind, calls men and women to similar ways of living. There is nothing so inspiring as its vistas, so calming, peaceful, and awesome as its oceans, so nourishing as its abundant crops, so wonderful as its sunrises and sunsets, so humbling as its threatening storms, and so shocking as its endless varieties of animals, flowers, and trees. For a reflective person there is not much randomness about this world. If we immerse ourselves in its wonders we cannot but think of who we are, why we are here, and what is our role and contribution.

A leader who appreciates the world and senses its beauty and wonder can feel called to contribute to a new world order, *a reordering of the world to serve the common good.* He or she can see the harmony of the world, the interrelationship and mutual dependence of all parts, the abundance of its never ending gifts. The world is a reflection of God's generosity and love—it is total gift with no charge. It is an image of the gifts and challenges of leadership; it is a teacher or guru of the needed qualities of leadership. A leader with the gift of appreciation can see in the world the various seasons of life, perceive how all things can move in unison, and celebrate how all creation discloses the beauty and grace that all life should reflect. A great spiritual leader appreciates the depth of the world's generosity and can feel called to open his or her heart to build a better world, to care for the environment, to work so that its abundance can be shared justly, to enjoy creation in all its beauty and excitement.

When a leader has the chance to see and appreciate the Matterhorn in all its splendor, or a pod of orca whales in the ocean off Alaska, or a brilliant sunset over the Pacific, or animals in the wild, that leader becomes a different person. He or she learns that *creation offers refreshment and healing, it is uplifting, inspirational, and awesome.* It offers its abundant generosity to everyone without discrimination. He or she also becomes aware of the need of attentiveness and care for this world that can be abused, degraded, and destroyed when leadership loses its direction and vision. He or she sees the world differently, sees himself or herself differently, and sees the human community differently. Appreciating the wonders of the world changes a person. Let us appreciate our world, be grateful for our home, and learn from the many lessons it offers us.

4. Listen to Pope Francis' challenges to care for the world

In 2015, Pope Francis wrote his letter to the world community on the care we should all show to our common home, the world (Encyclical Letter, *Laudato Si*). It is a wonderful document, full of challenges to all of us on how to take care of our planet. We have seen that appreciation is not a passive quality but a very active one that demands our involvement. These challenges form the basis for appreciating our world in wonder and awe and form a special teaching for spiritual leaders.

1. *Be aware of the problems.* Let us become more aware of our united concern for the health of our world. Nothing in the world is indifferent to us. We share life and we are sustained by our world. Our natural and social environments have been damaged, and we have models of production, consumption, and structures of power which lead to dysfunctional situations in our world. Each of us must acknowledge the great or small ecological damage we cause. Unless we see change in

humanity's approach to creation we will only be dealing with symptoms.

2. *Repent*. Our attitudes to the world are sinful and this calls for repentance from all involved. The violence in our own hearts is reflected in the way we plunder the earth, exploit, destroy, and degrade it. Many of us often see the world only for immediate use and consumption. We destroy the human environment, seeing it as our property for our exclusive use. Some people obstruct every effort at change, placing their confidence in technology. So, many feel free to disfigure, destroy, and contaminate the world. May we repent of these failures.

3. *Respond together*. We must unite with people of good will and respond together to the problems we have created. We need a new universal solidarity. Pursuing an integral ecology is at the heart of what is human. The world is God's gift to us all; it is a joyful mystery to be contemplated with gladness and praise. This awareness affects the way we treat the world and the choices which determine our behavior. Let us strive to confront this crisis together. We need strong responses that can face up to the special interests of economic powers. Unfortunately, we have already done enormous damage, and even now we lack cultural awareness, appropriate leadership, an acceptance of ecological debt, and legal frameworks for action. Instead we see ethical degradation, and constant excuses. Let us direct our responses to these problems.

4. *Dialogue*. Let us open a new dialogue with all people of good will about how to shape the future of our planet. This must become the basis for an ethical and spiritual journey that will reflect our unique place as human beings in our common home that we all share. We must dialogue on these issues with

all men and women who seek a better future for our planet. We need honesty in our dialogue. There is growing need for new national and local policies, politics that give priority to human life and fulfillment, and transparency in decision-making. To this we should add dialogue between religion and science.

5. *Face up to the consequences of our actions.* We must see the consequences of our actions. We have inflicted our world with pollution, climate change, global inequality, and constant waste. Our throwaway culture has led to a lack of water, a loss of biodiversity, and sickness that we inflict on ourselves and future generations. While many of our contemporaries try to conceal the symptoms of global harm and mask the problems in denial, we must call for a change of lifestyle, especially in our attitudes to production and consumption, otherwise we will see increase in global warming, rise in sea levels, and further destruction. Let us regularly look at the consequences of our actions.

6. *Focus on the quality of human life.* Our way of understanding human life and activity is out of line. Unfortunately, modern developments have not preserved the priority of human life, and now we have exploitation, overcrowding, unhealthy local environments, and poor housing. So, we must strive for integral improvements in the quality of human life. We must focus on the common good and justice. We are overwhelmed by deteriorization, pollution, congestion, and health concerns. The emphasis on consumption by a few produces an attitude of treating others like the disposable of society. All this must stop, and we must give precedence to the quality of human life.

7. *Be attentive to human degradation.* Environmental degradation is related to human and social degradation. We

see global inequality where the poorest suffer the most. Some of our leaders seem unaware of the suffering in the world caused by their decisions. In fact, many powerful countries maintain poor ones in poverty, with their disproportionate use of natural resources and imposition of excessive foreign debt. We must think about how the world can be different. This also means identifying the links between environmental degradation and the decline in quality of human life and the breakdown of society.

8. *Appreciate the mystery of the universe.* The earth is entrusted to us all and we must respect and appreciate the laws of nature given by the all-powerful Creator, and in our own way continue the work of creation. Humans must cultivate the abilities to protect the world. Every creature has its own purpose in the harmony of creation. Every creature has its own value and significance. Creation is a sign of God's goodness without measure. Creation is a constant source of wonder and awe, and appreciating creation we can rise to praise the Creator of this wonderful abundance.

9. *Give priority to the common good.* The way we treat our universe overflows in the way we treat each other, with love or cruelty. Humans have a tremendous responsibility for the world. Yes, they must look after the world, but their primary concern must be for other human beings. This requires concern, tenderness, and compassion for every human being. We must fight against human trafficking, all lack of concern for the poor, sick, and elderly, and every form of abuse. Our focus must be on the common good since the world is for everyone and the destination of the goods of this world must be for every human being. The earth is essentially a shared inheritance and its fruits are meant to benefit everyone.

10. *Develop an ecological education and spirituality.* When people are self-centered their greed increases. This is happening as our world becomes a seedbed for collective selfishness. But accumulation never satisfies the human heart. We must move away from collective selfishness and bring pressure to bear on centers of political, economic, and social power that they make a genuine commitment to change. Moreover, in our contemporary society, our information age, genuine self-examination, dialogue, and sincere encounters are blocked out by data overload. We need a profound interior conversion and then we must develop new lifestyles that include new habits, and together form an ecology of daily life. Ecological education always becomes social education. It is not just our natural environment that is under threat but also our historic, artistic, and cultural patrimony. We must learn how to live wisely.

Pope Francis hopes that leaders will show awareness, repentance, organized response, dialogue, and responsibility towards the problems of our world. Moreover, he calls leaders to face the consequences of their decisions, to focus on the quality of human development, and to assess the impact of human degradation. He goes on to insist that leaders stress genuine appreciation for God's gift of the world, give priority to the common good, and develop a spirituality that includes appreciation for our world.

This chapter calls leaders to appreciate the world in wonder and awe—attitudes that lead to a deeper level of life, commitment, and service. Few have these qualities but daily life that includes appreciation and attentiveness to people and organizational development make a difference in the dedication of truly exceptional leaders.

> *Points for reflection and meditation*
> - *In what ways do you constantly show appreciation for others?*
> - *Is your daily life immersed in trivia or can you distinguish important leadership moments from the clutter of noisy irrelevancies?*
> - *How would you like to change your daily pace of living; what would you like to be doing that you are not?*
> - *What do you learn from the world around you?*
> - *Which of Pope Francis' challenges speak to your heart?*

CHAPTER FIVE

IDENTIFY YOUR MOTIVATING CONVICTIONS

"To thine own self be true... Thou canst not then be false to anyone" (Polonius in *Hamlet*)

Men and women of spiritual sensitivity recognize that their leadership is a personal call or vocation in life. Situations of leadership are not the result of blind chance. No one is born to be a leader. Rather, there comes a moment when a person realizes he or she is someone or something different than before, and now has an important role in the service of others. However, the awareness of a vocation to leadership is above all a very personal experience, an appreciation of having a specific and unique task in this world. Awareness of this sense of being called is a powerful impetus to quality leadership. The vocation to leadership does not refer only to a task and responsibility, but it is a choice related to personal identity—who one wants to be and what kind of leader one chooses to be. This is a new style of life that results from this new perception of one's role, purpose, and destiny in society. At a time when many in leadership positions are adrift from their values, tossed here and there by the whim of the day or the pressures of their uninformed followers, leaders who have grown through authentic leisure, peaceful recollection, nurturing silence, and increased appreciation of others and the world, can give witness to what leadership can become. This leadership can be lived in any part of society, in any area of specialty and at any level in an organization.

The leadership of reflective men and women is affected by awareness of their call and by the quality of their spiritual lives as a result of that call. Such leaders appreciate the basic values that motivate their lives. Out of these values comes an awareness of an enduring purpose in life, and this leads one to appreciate one's destiny in this world—a destiny to be a transformed, spiritual leader always at the service of others. This sense of one's identity results from the inward journey into one's heart to be alone in recollection, silence, and contemplative reflection where one quietly discovers one's personal identity and place in life. This then grows and evolves over time—often with the aid of colleague, spouse, or friend—into an appreciation of one's leadership calling. Such an individual lives from the inner spiritual core out to others with a unique style of leadership. This deepening appreciation of call includes acceptance of one's gifts and mission. Such a leader accepts his or her role and stature, even realizing it is a gift for others. This is part of a fascinating and frightening mystery, and a leader must have the courage to be the person he or she is capable of being.

1. State your purpose in life

Anyone who wishes to exercise effective leadership must frequently pause to reflect in times of leisure, recollection, silence, and wonder, to rethink and rediscover the *importance of a personal call or vocation* to leadership. One does not become a better leader by simply increasing one's knowledge, or learning new behaviors, or participating in new helpful experiences. Leadership is a response to a vocation heard in the depths of one's heart as a result of a mature inner consciousness. Leadership is based on a transformed pattern of life in which the leader is motivated by a set of core values faithfully lived out with discipline, fortitude, and integrity. Such a leader is moved and motivated by an inward certainty concerning these values that give meaning to life.

Everyone acts out of motivating values, some good and some bad. Some people never articulate these values, and it is left to others to recognize them for good or ill. However, it is desirable that a leader becomes aware of what these values are, sort and prioritize them, select or reject some, purify them, and see how they come together to define a greater purpose in life. Outstanding leadership emerges from a life that has become conscious of itself and its purpose. A visionary leader constantly searches for the connections between doing a good job each day and being faithful to a perceived purpose in life. While some organizations and leaders today are always lowering the bar on values, a dedicated leader, motivated by significant, special priorities, seeks always to raise society's commitment to values, notably integrity and service.

This value-centered and purpose driven *leadership always grows into love* in three ways: a love to be more, to be for, and to be with. In other words, such a leader in being faithful to his or her purpose in life seeks to be more fully alive—to be the best one is capable of being. Such a leader in fidelity to purpose in life seeks to focus the whole of leadership and life on being for others in service. These spiritual leaders who are motivated by such values focus on being and doing all in union with others for the common good. So, they love to be more, to be for, and to be with.

Great leaders have standards for their own sake. They faithfully devote their knowledge, gifts, and hopes to personal growth and to *promoting the core values that guide their lives*. They appreciate that they have no future unless they add value. This pursuit of values inevitably leads to the pursuit of love, and ultimately for believers to the pursuit of God. Such leaders act as a kind of soul for human society, always calling it to the best it is capable of being. These leaders are passionate about what they do and their passion becomes contagious, as others are drawn to a deeper awareness of a shared common purpose in life. So, the leader's passionate pursuit of purpose attracts and energizes others, helps them find their own meaning and purpose in life, and inspires them in their daily dedication. Spiritual leaders who pursue their identified vision must sustain their commitment by humility and ongoing learning whether cognitive or experiential. These two aspects of their leadership will serve to counter any arrogance and instead introduce a little fear, a readiness to always learn, and a willingness to be open to guidance from other leaders who like themselves seek to be faithful to a greater goal.

2. Acknowledge what you believe

Once a leader focuses on the major, motivating convictions, it naturally leads to a broader *awareness of one's destiny*. Why am I convinced of certain values? Why do I act in the way I do? What do I think is my purpose in life? There follows an even more demanding question, what do I really believe about life, my place in it, and the reason for my leadership? So, from motivating convictions and reason for living one can go on to acknowledge personal beliefs; thus making conscious what lies unconscious in one's conviction and purpose. In the quality times of quiet reflection a leader can ask what he or she believes about self, others, community, leadership, the meaning of life, and God.

Great spiritual leaders go deeper in questioning themselves about convictions, purpose, and even belief systems and must ask what led to all this. At the basis of people's profound convictions, sense of purpose, and beliefs, there is generally, if not always, a *personal experience that changed the leader's life*. Perceptive leaders seek to identify this transforming experience that led them to live in the way they do. It is always an experience they have had and never a collection of intellectual convictions about leadership. A spiritual leader places his or her faith in this experience. It is not something we can achieve but a transformative experience that comes to people who have prepared themselves in quiet times, recollection, silence, and wonder and have prepared their hearts to be emptied of false values and filled with new ones. This experience in which a leader places his or her faith is an experience that happens to us and that we cannot deny. For a spiritual leader it is an experience that brings inner knowledge and a life-giving vision of one's role and destiny in the world.

This experience can be some special enlightenment in a moment's intuition into a personal or world event—the death of a friend, the total love of a spouse, the pain and suffering of a neighbor, the greed and corruption of a politician or businessperson, the struggles of the poor, the impact of war, and so on. It can also be the experience of a power or presence in life that one has never previously experienced, or one's sense of helplessness without some experience of redemption, or one's awareness of one's own insignificance. In all these cases *a reflective leader must confront the experience* and ask what it personally means. Besides these moments of shocking awareness there are some other levels of awareness that affect a leader little by little over prolonged periods until one can no longer ignore them.

In everyone's life there are *moments that are very special* and they give birth to convictions and faith. These experiences give us insight into the meaning of our lives. They are not only memorable but also transforming, and after such an experience our lives can never be the same again. It seems that we touch something, even someone, beyond the normal horizons of life, and the experience gives us insight beyond all previous knowing. This experience is the basis of faith and a challenge to spiritual growth; it is a call, a personal vocation that clarifies our purpose in life and the meaning of our leadership.

This *experience beyond the normal horizons of life* is very personal, and no one else can have this experience for us. In fact, we cannot even control it ourselves. It happens to us. We can only recognize it as a gift and receive it with gratitude. We cannot earn this experience, but we can prepare ourselves for it through reflection, peaceful attitudes, and openness to life's richness and beauty. We can also train ourselves to become people of stillness, inspiration, concentration, and silence and thus ready ourselves for insight beyond the normal and natural.

When we catch a glimpse into a world of realities beyond the usual horizons it leads to a conversion, to *a new way of knowing and understanding life,* and to a new way of knowing and loving ourselves and others. At the same time, the transforming experience itself becomes our guide, as we live out the values we learned in our experience. An experience such as this leads to the conviction that we learn more about ourselves and our ultimate destiny in the abandonment to such a special experience than in the accumulated knowledge of the past. In this conversional transformation we focus our spiritual commitment, we grasp before all else a new understanding of ourselves as part of a grander plan that links our lives with others and with a new horizon beyond normal aspects of life.

This experience calls us to live with a new sense of personal vocation and dedication. *We are primarily the people who must be accountable for what we experience.* We appreciate the call to spiritual growth and the challenge to take all necessary steps to achieve it. We can no longer stand still and do nothing. In quiet, recollection, silence, and wonder we enter a special moment. We must take these special moments of insight into our ultimate purpose in life seriously and never let them pass unanswered.

3. Live with convictions

A leader who knows his or her direction in life and has encountered a sense of destiny in a deep and transforming experience in which he or she now has profound faith *longs to share these values with others.* Two convictions characterize such leaders: the integrity of the message and their absolute awareness that it is their destiny to proclaim and embody it for others. Contemporary leaders of this kind know that they are, and must be, intimately faithful to the values they have experienced and that now guide their lives; they must make conscious decisions based on what they believe. This world of ours is not a very agreeable place to live in, and a leader must stand out against its values, for leadership is frequently counter-cultural. However, the leader feels compelled to promote the purity of the message that has been seen to be his or her purpose and destiny in this world.

A leader's convictions form a vision and this vision determines what needs to be done in the present because of how the leader sees the future. That is exactly what a prophet does—tells the community how they ought to live in the present because of what is seen as a desired future for the community. *A prophet speaks out of conviction.* So much so that contemporary spiritual leadership has a prophetical component to it. A prophet knows that the whole of life is given over to proclaiming a vision. Such a leader will do anything and everything to bring the vision to reality, carrying out the mission with both patience and urgency. Above all the prophet must be authentic, knowing that leadership is not about improving one's own status, but about interpreting and implementing a vision. For such a leader everything done must reflect the vision that is based on convictions, and on a personal transforming experience.

Prophetical leaders must be made of the right stuff for there is too much money, greed, power, sex, and control in modern society that these temptations overwhelm leaders in all walks of life. In presenting a vision of the common good, prophetical leaders must not only be inspired by their own convictions and faith but also inspire others with *conviction that a new spirit of human interaction is possible*—their message rings with freshness, integrity, power, and hope. They must stay the course whatever the cost. Prophetical leaders are marginal, not part of the mainstream of managerial leadership. Many people will find their bold message too controversial for contemporary organizational life. Unfortunately we have become too accustomed to things as they are and have been, and we need courage to risk something different. But the purpose of prophetical leadership is more radical than social change, for it is part of an integrated vision for humanity; a vision of which the spiritual leader has caught a glimpse in reflecting on his or her convictions, purpose, destiny, and faith.

Prophetical leaders are creative, as they *challenge people to reshape the future of organizations* in spite of the lurking danger from those who want to preserve the status quo. This can be a dangerous undertaking, for the selfishly powerful do not like to change what they can use to their own advantage. As the prophetical leader looks to the vision that guides life and leadership, he or she challenges people to believe things can and must be different. This means dismantling dominant structures, providing alternative ways for people to live in society, and introducing new relationships in communities.

So, a prophetical *leader must turn his or her convictions and faith into practical involvement.* Vision is always a mere dream unless it is implemented. The prophet's compelling vision must include dedicated service; in other words, a sense of mission lived in values. The values do not create the vision, but they measure the rightness of the vision. If the prophet can enthusiastically persuade others to pursue the hope-filled vision, it will attract commitment, energize followers, create meaning in workers' lives, establish standards of excellence, and bridge the gap between the present and the future. Although the vision is based on the leader's profound convictions and faith, he or she does not own the vision. Rather it is constantly evolving with the help of others. The vision is based on profound convictions and an experience of faith; it is shared with others and has the inherent power to draw others to its goals. However, there will be many obstacles in the way, but faith must be lived out each day with courageous perseverance.

4. Build your life on ten fundamental convictions

Great leaders live each day motivated by a series of convictions that are part of their lives as a result of profound experiences they have or have had or of a new awareness of their role in the world. Some leaders, because of their personal experiences will have different convictions than others. However, below are given some of the basic common convictions that motivate great leaders, and readers can modify the list from their own vision, experience, and commitment.

1. *Always do more.* We need leaders who are willing to do more, stand for more, be more, and, yes, even suffer more in order to achieve more. The greedy, the controllers, the abusers, the power-hungry still seem to determine the direction of organizational life. We need leaders of conviction who will present society with what ought to be done to have just organizational and professional lives. Leaders today must be men and women who will do more and go beyond professional commitment to discretionary commitment that is the singular requirement for great change. We need leaders with generous hearts who will seek to make a difference to other people's lives and give of their all to enable organizations and society achieve their ends in a hope-filled vision.

2. *Live with integrity.* Integrity requires courage to speak the truth, to accept one's own independence and autonomy, to honestly present the implications of a vision, and to faithfully persevere in the demands of a vision even when it means standing alone. Integrity always needs to be complemented with humility, appreciation of honest doubt, and healthy skepticism. Integrity is primarily an inner self-knowledge but also refers to followers' perception that leaders' values and actions match their words. It is the spiritual discipline of always speaking the truth, of making sure we do what we claim we will do, and of being ready to hold on to the course of action. When a person has integrity he or she gains the trust of others.

3. *Put other people first.* Leadership must include the conviction that one must emphasize the movement away from self to self-transcendence with the goal of stressing the central importance of others. Spiritual leaders focus not on their own goals but community goals because they believe in people. Changing focus from self to others begins with simple everyday

practices, deliberately appreciating some positive quality of someone else and taking no one for granted, listening carefully to others' communications, giving credit to others whenever possible, showing appreciation and gratitude, and recognizing their personal gifts and achievements. Furthermore, focusing on others means valuing others, delegating authority to them, encouraging them to participate in decision-making, getting out of their way when they accept responsibility, and celebrating their successes.

4. *Offer hope.* The vision of hope that is the primary motivator of exceptional leadership consists in more than the futuring skills of leadership. It is a faith-filled vision of our hopes for humanity as a whole and for each individual in particular. This hope reveals who we are called to be, and it opens our hearts to the promises of God. Then, such hope challenges us to live in light of this future in which we believe. Hope reflects the true inner convictions of a person. It results from conversion and is proof of faith. For such a person hope is the source of life, as it is the source of leadership.

5. *Present a vision.* A vision articulates what an individual or organization wishes to become. Having vision essentially implies seeing what others do not see. Vision includes the ability to see the big picture, all sides of an issue. Increasingly, it means having insight into present realities and capitalizing on some immediate perspective that others do not appreciate. More importantly nowadays, vision is not only seeing in a way others do not see, it is a deliberate decision to look at things in a new way. It starts with one's basic values and one's deliberately identified purpose in life. These two facets of one's personality together form one's philosophy of life. These lead to one's sense of mission or destiny, and out of this comes goals and strategies.

6. *Share and collaborate.* This conviction includes the idea that collaboration is not a way of doing something more efficiently but a way of being an organization more authentically. Collaboration requires friendship where love and mutual respect show in the conviction that we are moving to a common vision and would be incomplete without each other. It requires love and humility, interior freedom, selflessness, and a desire to seek the truth and serve the common good with the conviction that all are gifted to contribute to the vision we share.

7. *Confront injustice.* A great leader is convinced that he or she must bear the burdens of the oppressed and challenge the injustices of oppressive individuals and structures. He or she feels impelled to denounce injustices wherever discovered and develop goals and strategies to uproot injustice. Confronting injustice requires prudence, patience, and firm determination to take whatever opportunities occur. A good leader will insist that values play a major role in all aspects of organizational life.

8. *Maintain support systems.* When a spiritual leader feels called to dedicate his or her whole life in the service of others, then he or she will need to be prudent enough to arrange a series of strong supports that can help maintain one's dedication. These supports enrich leadership but also every aspect of life, helping the leader become a better person, spouse, friend, parent, and member of community. The following supports should be kept in mind. The leader should develop strategies against excessive stress, align leadership with values, and create space in personal life. He or she must make sure to find a supportive community, seek enlightenment from a strong personal faith, and benefit from becoming a contemplative leader. Such a leader should accept

the power that is offered in leadership, be aware of stages in growth as a leader, and develop enthusiasm for the journey. Finally, he or she must clarify the image of God who constantly draws one to leadership.

9. *Remember vocation.* The call to be a great leader means being a magnanimous person of truthfulness and integrity who can break down barriers and release the potential of followers. This conviction leads to adult leadership, and it requires passion, boldness, and courage. The call is a powerful invitation to become a significant person in community. It is not for the weak-hearted or partially identified. It is a way of life. The person who accepts this call will never be the same again, and neither will the people with whom he or she works, lives, and shares life.

10. *Be aware of transcendent values.* Many leaders now are everyday mystics—they appreciate the transcendent in leadership. They know intangibles are as important as tangibles. Such a leader is a person of interiority and hope and builds the vision on what he or she has experienced of respect, justice, compassion, community, mutuality, and love. In times of prayerful reflection, such a leader encounters the call of the living God, challenging him or her to be faithful to a new vision. A spiritual leader is open to the transcendent and finds a new way of being a leader. In contemplative reflection, he or she discovers God's vision of how a leader serves humanity. Certainly, the spiritual leader realizes at depth that leadership is a personal vocation, and this awareness leads to a new way of interacting with others.

Points for reflection and meditation

- *Which are the key convictions that motivate your life?*
- *Why do you think you are in this world? What is your purpose in life?*
- *What is the most important experience that changed your life and what did you learn from that experience?*
- *Do you live with integrity?*
- *Who helps you to maintain your convictions?*

CHAPTER SIX

THINK ABOUT OTHERS' PAIN AND SUFFERING

"Out of suffering have emerged the strongest souls" (Kahlil Gibran)

We have so far considered five key experiences that transform the lives and values of leaders. When leaders give themselves to these practices they enter a new level of awareness about life, other people, and leadership. In this chapter we ask leaders to develop a deeper sensitivity to the suffering and pain of others. This increased sensitivity affects a leader's judgment, fosters compassion, and makes a leader more human.

A reflective leader understands that our world is anything but perfect. We are surrounded by human pain and suffering, much of it caused by human beings, part of it unanswered because some self-centered people have other selfish priorities. The common experience of suffering connects human beings from all over the world, but common responses to suffering would bring us even closer together. Unfortunately, many even inflict suffering in God's name, and their blasphemy destroys their own and others' faith. Reflective leaders who feel called to the ongoing transformation of people and of our world know they must confront suffering and alleviate pain. Remembering suffering is an important strategy for spiritual leaders. Dealing with it shows where their values of mind and heart lie—focused on self or on others. It shows they are moving from self-centeredness to self-transcendence. Focusing on suffering reminds us that a leader's life must include healing and redemption, the removal of undesirable obstacles, and the search for wholeness. Suffering can be physical, psychological, moral, or spiritual. Healing will include a sense of well-being, restoration of human dignity, and clarification of the meaning of life and of death. Confronting suffering and alleviating pain is an integral part of spiritual leadership.

1. Remember others' pain

Our world does not like to think about suffering, and sometimes we ourselves pass over it. We say we must bring closure and move on. But *we need to savor suffering*, whether in our own lives or in others', both personally and institutionally, and we must make other people confront sufferings, interrupting the peaceful and deliberate ignoring of others' suffering. To suggest that the happiness and painless existence of a few at the top will trickle down to bring happiness and the alleviation of suffering for the poor, sick, helpless masses is itself an example of the sickness that infects society. In fact, the alleviation of suffering is blocked by sinful, selfish acts of individuals for sure, but, the major blocks to remembering suffering come from attitudes that, while immoral, have become the normal order of the day. These disordered positions become part of our culture, our normal ways of viewing things. They are rationalized, justified, and even religiously supported—all efforts to anaesthetize us against suffering. Thinking about suffering is a responsibility of leadership and challenges leaders to come up with new priorities in our way of thinking about people and their suffering and hopes.

Leaders must actively and *courageously remember suffering*. We can never identify suffering only with some unfortunate others, for there is suffering in everyone's life. Clearly, some suffer immensely and unjustly, but suffering is part of the human condition, and we can all relate to it—it is part of who we are. Even those who inflict suffering on others are sick and in need of healing. Certainly, it takes courage to remember suffering. The horrors of Auschwitz were inflicted by human beings, mainly Christians, who made us see the total moral depravity to which human beings can fall, and this moral depravity continues in many ways today. Recent natural disasters with entire cities destroyed sees much of the blame going to builders, planners, enforcers, who failed in their duties, causing death and destruction and revealing the consequences of cheating. We have witnessed enormous greed in business and finance that has ruined the lives of millions while the guilty perpetrators walk away with the wealth they have stolen from their clients. It takes courage to remember suffering for some memories can be dangerous. When we look at suffering it can be a shocking experience, reminding us of what humanity can become. This frightening experience can change us from being selfish to selfless. It can challenge us to think about ourselves as we stand before God and about the true values of humanity. Faced with the horrors of suffering we are called to live the values felt deep in our hearts. Remembering suffering can transform our lives, bringing a spirit of humility, solidarity, compassion, and community. If we fail to remember suffering we can become arrogant, hard-hearted, selfish, and inhuman. Dealing with suffering is clearly an essential challenge of leadership.

Leaders of spiritual dedication, caught up in suffering can *draw on their inner strength, endurance, hope, and love.* As their hearts go out to others who suffer, they feel a profound sadness for those who cause it, and they admire those who live peacefully through suffering. They can sense how good the absence of suffering can be and determine to remove it from the lives of others. Suffering is anything that negatively affects well-being, and there is no satisfactory explanation for all situations. Suffering is linked to the problem of evil, the mystery of life, and the incomprehensibility of God.

Responding to suffering means a new view of the world and of what it means to be human and to be a leader. Suffering always calls out for healing, for it just seems wrong. When suffering is inflicted deliberately or results as a consequence of one's self-centered choices it is always contrary to humanity. *Responding to suffering means a conversion*—a change of heart, a new outlook on life. Spiritual leaders must look to the basic values they hold as a result of reflection. From these basic values there emerges a purpose in life. This philosophy of life gives rise to a sense of purpose and destiny. All these elements together form a vision of life—a vision that sees suffering as an aberration, whether it is one's own suffering or someone else's. Responding must eventually lead to action, but first a leader must take a stance against all suffering, making sure this new outlook resulting from conversion leads to thinking and living differently. Attitudes to suffering have a special place in human growth, for one's approach to suffering makes one more human or less human. So, responding is intimately linked to who one is and who one can become. This response is part of spirituality. Attitudes to suffering are not only focused through faith and hope, but particularly in love. Love guides our approach to suffering at every stage.

A leader responds to suffering first and foremost with a new vision and understanding of the importance of *confronting suffering as part of a leadership response*. However, a leader must then move to a call for action, aligning behavior with values and becoming actively involved in removing situations that cause suffering. One can actively and deliberately withhold support from individuals or organizations that cause suffering or do nothing to alleviate suffering even though they could. So, one can withhold support from unethical organizations that cause suffering. Some groups that support war and those who finance them, some banking systems and practices that discriminate, some healthcare and pharmaceutical companies whose policies of pricing and of withholding help lead to suffering, some political subgroups who negatively affect the poor and unfortunate—one can target all these for inflicting suffering on others. Current injustices in business, healthcare, education, and law are the same as they have been for years, and we can actively oppose leaders who do harm or do nothing.

A leader can also become more socially and politically involved in order to work to reduce suffering, supporting movements that challenge injustice and alleviate suffering. Thus, one can support movements for women's justice, healthcare for the poor at home and throughout the world, movements for children's welfare, safety, and education, movements that support victims of all kinds of abuse. Leaders must work for what is not only legal, but what is fair, what is just, and what is in keeping with a vision based on motivating values.

2. Accept the pain in leadership

A leader is a person who has the courage to move forward through trials and setbacks and is strengthened by the conviction that he or she can help others even those who oppose everything. Great leaders are not known for the absence of conflict and struggle in their lives but rather for how they deal with adversity and pain. *Dealing with pain and suffering is a part of leadership.* Great leaders bring their care, watchfulness, and love to others' struggles, sorrow, and pain. A leader motivated by values learned in reflection can help others deal with the mysteries of life and pain and bring spiritual empowerment to others in their confronting of suffering. Sometimes a leader just feels a lump in his or her inner self when seeing the horrors others face. A leader's call to transform other peoples' lives is heard loudly when confronted with suffering, and the ability to help others bear their pain is a highly valued spiritual gift—not just endurance, but a love-motivated gift.

Pain and distress are part of a leader's life too. *A leader has to suffer a lot to get anything done* for the good of others. Just setting a new direction in one's life and leadership is stressful. A leader abandons a past thought to be fine and launches out to an unknown future, and there is always adversity. A leader experiences at the same time hope in a new choice and regret for former ways of leading. The conversional experience of setting a new direction brings insecurity, darkness, and a threat of lost good things. However, every worthwhile step in leadership development has its price to pay, and one must die to certain forms of superficial leadership in order to move to spiritual leadership.

A leader who passes through a conversional experience *moves from a set of old values to a set of new ones* and feels that the ground beneath him or her is giving way. Having seen that there is more to leadership than one first thought, the leader stops seeing things in one way and starts seeing them in a new way. This experience at first shocks the leader, leaving him or her discouraged at having spent perhaps a long time dedicated to the wrong values. The leader-to-be savors the pain of this loss, for he or she must become convinced in the depths of soul that former values are inadequate. As the leader struggles to set a new direction in life, one accepts the pain and loss, knowing that only when one is truly emptied of false values can one be filled with new and transforming ones.

Accepting the distress associated with one's conversion in leadership helps one to help others in their pain. Leadership includes this dimension of healing offered to others who experience adversity. Memory of pain, solidarity in pain, and listening to the stories of those who suffer are three tasks that leaders can practice as people of faith to help them improve their spiritual leadership. Such leaders, caught up in others' experiences can draw on their inner strength, endurance, hope, and love, as they long to bring healing to others and to organizations. *Their hearts go out to others who suffer*, they feel a profound sadness for those who cause it, and they admire those who live peacefully through the trials that working in organizations can bring. They can sense how good the absence of suffering can be and determine to remove it from the lives of others.

Responding to the pain of others means a new view of the world and of *what it means to be huma*n. When suffering is inflicted deliberately or results as a consequence of a leader's self-centered choices it is always contrary to humanity. Responding means a conversion—a change of heart, a new outlook on life. Leaders must think about the causes of suffering and whether they are the cause of suffering for anyone else. They should reflect on whether there is anything in their lives and work that causes difficulties for others. Accepting pain is an integral part of setting a new direction in life.

3. Enter the painful transition of leadership

When we examine a leader's human maturity and spiritual growth we find there are *two essential stages in a leader's personal devel*opment, separated from each other by one of the most profound spiritual experiences of his or her life. However, while both stages offer good elements, most leaders spend all their lives in the first stage, do not have the courage to go further, know no better, and will never change. They work with dedicated and patient endurance, unenlightened by hope, and grounded in what can only be seen by the eyes. It is better to refer to these dedicated people as inspired managers, since what they do affects primarily the organization and not its people.

A few leaders move to a second stage, especially the reflective leaders of whom we have spoken in previous chapters. Their work transforms not only the organization but also each of its members, individually and as a community. In the first stage an inspired manager acts as if everything depends on him or her. This kind of leader fills his or her every minute with effort, planning, programming, strategizing, and evaluating. The leader in stage two reflects on life values as a source for a different kind of leadership. He or she treasures quiet time and an effortless approach to life. Such a leader accepts weakness and values leisure, recollection, silence, and a sense of wonder, convinced of benefiting from being controlled by a greater power than self.

These two stages in human maturity and spiritual growth form the basis for a leader's spiritual development. They are closely linked together. The first is an active effort-filled stage and is necessary for everyone and always precedes the contemplative and receptive experiences of stage two. *Stage two includes two focuses*; first, a moving forward to new experiences, a sense of being drawn to immerse oneself in a vision we have seen; second, stage two also includes a refocusing on stage one but with the attitudes of stage two. The spiritual, reflective leader we have described does not neglect the basic leadership values and skills of stage one but transforms them with the aid of a new awareness that comes in interior renewal and transformation.

Spiritual leaders are men and women of presence who *bring a new meaning to everything they do*; to work, to relationships, to ethics and justice, to institutional purpose and mission. Their leadership builds on insight, intuition, artistic creativity, poetry, friendship, and community. They not only treasure what can be measured but also the untapped resources of transcendent values. For them, spirituality is an intimate part of leadership excellence. They are men and women of wisdom, a little like the sages of old.

The transition from stage one to stage two is painful for a leader. It is *an experience of the pain and darkness of leadership*. It is a crisis of confidence in what the leader has so far been doing; it is a sense of loss that former successes no longer mean anything; it is the death of past values and the willingness to let them die for they are based on a vision that is too small. The leader who goes through this spiritual experience of passage from a set of old values to a set of new values feels the ground beneath him or her is giving way. One grasps that there is more to life than meeting goals and objectives, increasing profits, satisfying shareholders, marketing a successful product or service. People, community, justice, others' fulfillment, love, and changing the values of society are all more important. All good leaders achieve the former, great spiritual leaders also achieve the latter, and so are filled with hope.

We desperately need people willing to endure the pain of this transition in leadership and to participate in the transformation. Certainly, leadership must change! The transition from stage one to stage two is an experience of darkness, a dark night when a person cannot see because of the brightness of illumination. In other words, in this important transition, one cannot see—not because there is no light, but because there is too much light. The transition to a new level of leadership is an experience of darkness that enables the leader to *stop seeing in one way and to start seeing things in a new way.* This is part of doing away with the idols of organizational life, of getting rid of the gods of prior visions of leadership. These experiences at first shock us, leave us discouraged, and give us a sense of failure in having spent life dedicated to the wrong values. A leader must savor the pain of this loss for he or she must become convinced in the depths of soul that former values are inadequate.

This is a breakthrough experience, an immersion in a mystery beyond us, and it leads to clarity of vision, insightful responsiveness to the vision of promise, an expansion of the mind's perception, and insight into the realities of leadership and organizational life. It is a new knowledge. The transitional experience also brings peace, comfort, a healthy indifference, and hope. The leader no longer fears failure, since success comes from outside of self. The leader is alone in this experience, but it is the occasion of self-discovery and the answer to one's search for meaning in life. This transition is a letting go of the past and a purification of the arrogance, greed, and selfishness that taint leadership. It is a simple, intuitive, and immediate experience that manifests the obvious way things should be, and it bears no disagreement, it is the vision of promise and hope.

4. Lead in a world of suffering

A leader is always uncomfortable. Leaders deal with problems every day and so must be skilled at living with tension. A good leader feels drawn to leadership and repelled by it at the same time. He or she need to constantly reaffirm commitment and maintain hope. Such a leader knows difficulties are an integral part of leadership, can bear the pain and frustration being a leader brings, and can manage the discouragement, depression, and rejection that working with others produces. This leader looks for the good in all that happens, and reminds himself or herself of how often positive developments result from events that started out negatively. A reflective leader focuses heart on mission and recommits himself or herself to it and to all the struggles that are integral to its achievement.

Embrace pain and suffering. A reflective leader appreciates that suffering is an integral part of the life of a leader. Generally a person with a sense of destiny has gone through personal suffering and crisis which can often become a source of strength and gives the courage to continue. A good leader is conscious of the pain that surrounds an organization, never inflicts pain on co-workers, but embraces pain and suffering, accepts it while seeking to remove it from the lives of others. Leadership implies transforming life in spite of suffering. A leader is often the target of suffering and often has to ignore a lot of negativity, major doses of cynicism, and imposed constraints in order to get things done. If a leader is tempted to ask when will it all end, he or she must know it is a permanent part of leadership. In spite of the suffering a leader must struggle to energize others. Such a leader can be ready for constant change, take success or failure in stride, and face the future with passion, boldness, and courage.

Accept failure. If a leader wants to be successful then he or she must learn to live with failure and the pain it brings. A leader must not be anxious when the future does not yield all the success one hopes for but must remain calm and peaceful. A leader's joys and strengths are always linked to needs and miseries that also come along. Every day will have its pains and struggles, in fact, some experiences a leader must confront seem to suck the life out of a person. A good leader accepts the limits of his or her successes and thereby moves beyond them. A spiritual leader also appreciates the gifts of all and establishes a new approach to failure for others too, in fact, even welcomes it, knowing that anyone who wants to be successful must learn to fail and learn from failing.

Bring healing to organizations. There is an intimate link between leadership and healing. A spiritual leader focuses on integrated, holistic approaches to people and to organizations, removing what is sick and dysfunctional, bringing harmony, striving for wellness, and thus enriching the vision. A leader must first of all repair the harm of the past and the pain it caused. A spiritual leader is aware that organizations are often sick and dysfunctional, have harmful environments and structures, and become oppressive and destructive. There are many casualties of sick organizations that are filled with disharmony and lack of balance. All this needs healing too. Spiritual leaders should review their organizations and discern what needs healing. They should encourage all to live the vision with courage and perseverance. To this end they will cultivate a spirit of reconciliation and compassion in the whole community.

Remember some truths can only be seen in darkness. We live today in dark times and often a leader finds it difficult to come up with the right answers or is bombarded with answers that turn out to be superficial. Living in times of darkness when nothing seems clear can be a good experience, for darkness helps us block out partial answers, eliminate those which do harm, and challenge leaders to think things through more carefully. Darkness can be the beginning of newness of life which is like a dawn. In fact, one can even find what one is looking for even when you are not looking—answers just come effortlessly in dark times and in times of reflection. So, life can sometimes be better in darkness and leaders learn to trust times of darkness. What darkness does for us is do away with useless answers that come in partial light; so one can even say that enlightenment come in darkness. Nothing is ever so bright as when one comes out of darkness

Work with pathological leaders. In many organizations leader pathology is a serious problem and trying to collaborate with such unbalanced people is painful for leaders with values. Our world is complex and also sinful, and some of the worst situations are the result of the failure of public figures. Spiritual leaders are always living in the shadow of pathological leaders who have no sense of justice or dedication to service. Good leaders must maintain self-control and not accept the failures of others but rather offer an alternative way of being a leader in contemporary society.

Be joyful, optimistic, and enthusiastic. Joy, optimism, and enthusiasm are three interconnected concepts in the life of a spiritual leader who must struggle with the pains and suffering of our contemporary world. He or she needs to be vibrant, cheerful, full of interests, and excited about life. All leadership has its times of oppression, justified reactions of anger, and feelings of resentment. A leader has to put up with a lot of negativity and personal criticisms while trying to keep optimistic and to maintain positive motivation of others. Joy is an essential component of the life of a spiritual leader, preceding and concluding every stage in leadership. Optimism is the attitude of a leader who takes a hopeful view of things, expects positive outcomes, and looks forward to achieving good developments through leadership. Enthusiasm describes a leader who is guided by the values of God (en theos = in God) and can approach his or her work with confidence. These three qualities enable a leader to live with courageous patience, resilience, innovative thinking, openness to the future, and encouraging hope.

Points for reflection and meditation

- *Who are the people around you who seem to be in pain and what support do you offer them?*
- *Which are the pains that you must deal with in your leadership?*
- *Do you think you have matured as a leader? How is your leadership different today than it used to be?*
- *What role does failure play in your life and in the lives of your co-workers?*
- *Would others describe you as a joyful, optimistic, and enthusiastic leader?*

CHAPTER SEVEN

VALUE PEOPLE ABOVE ALL ELSE

"Train people well enough so they can leave; treat them well enough so they won't want to"
(Sir Richard Branston)

Good leadership always takes care of the tangible aspects of one's responsibility—product, service, revenue, budget, and so on. But good leaders complement these task-oriented aspects of leadership with interpersonal, people-oriented skills. Thus, gifts of mind find enrichment in gifts of heart. The former were often referred to as the hard issues of leadership whereas the latter were the soft issues. Moreover, in past decades, leaders' responsibilities emphasized the former whereas workers now largely take care of those themselves. Leaders' primary responsibilities today center on people—skills for team-building, empowerment, trust, delegation, appreciation, and so on. Good leaders commit themselves to people and their development above all else, and pursue this with purpose and passion.

Nothing of significance can be done by an organization unless the leader succeeds in harnessing the competencies and talents of its people. When a leader achieves this there follows a raising up of the spirit and commitment of individuals in the group and of the entire community together. The effects of such a transformation include heightened energy, a sense of personal and group well-being, and an enlarged sense of creativity. People become more willing to dialogue and make connections with each other, to sacrifice themselves for the common good, and to strive to make future hopes part of the present reality. These common commitments and shared vision lead people to a sense of peace, enthusiasm, and clarity of judgment in their actions on behalf of the organization's common goals.[4] Thus, when leaders value people above all else it has major impact throughout the organization.

1. Understand the consequences of neglecting others

This book offers leaders a series of reflections on which those who wish to be exceptional leaders can meditate. It would be great if readers would think deeply about these issues in the hope that they can move to a new set of convictions that can transform their lives. "How-to" books are fine for the inexperienced but insufficient for the new depth of conviction that is needed for conversion and transformation that can alone produce leadership that makes a difference to other people's lives. So, we have given time in previous chapters to appreciating the value of genuine leisure, recollection, and silence as solid foundations for a new set of attitudes for leadership. We have thought about the importance of a leader's sense of appreciation and wonder of the world and its people. We reflected on the need to articulate one's convictions, beliefs, and purpose in life. We stressed the value of understanding the part played by suffering in people's lives today and what should be a spiritual leader's response. This chapter and the next are critical to the fostering of great leadership, since *how one treats others makes the difference in what kind of leader one becomes*. However, the way we treat others does not depend on techniques or people skills—even though they help—but on deep convictions of mind and heart regarding our relationship to others.

In recent decades, we have witnessed a lot of selfishness, greed, and abusive attitudes to workers and to communities. Some managers clearly ignore, suppress, and intimidate co-workers. Some terminate workers and close down places of work with no consideration given to the suffering of people. Others have presided over failed organizations with worthless vision because they prefer to dry up and die rather than see others succeed. Thus, incompetent leaders cling to positions and jeopardize others' growth and success. Many who work closely together are poles apart, workers' valid opinions stifled and substituted with disagreement and neglect. What could be creative and redemptive becomes abortive and cynical. Workers' silence is equated with ignorance and their great ideas left unrecognized as pseudo-leaders bulldoze every idea except their own. *Many leaders do not seem to care about other people.* So much so, that Pope Francis speaks about the globalization of indifference.[5]

Some leaders today are excessively engrossed in their own advancement to the neglect of other people. *Many such leaders are intoxicated with selfishness* and view others as being in the way of their success. In fact, our consumer society uses people and sees this as a normal approach to life. There is so much consumerism and greed along with intense nastiness and even hate that we have become anesthetized to the just treatment of others. We need remedial training to get away from this, a reordering of our values towards others which starts with strenuous efforts against abusive attitudes to people.

There are a lot of false formulas for treating others. One thing is clear; *the human heart can never be satisfied in using others* but only when mutuality allows enrichment. We are left in poverty and insufficiency without others' enriching lives. Perhaps authentic Christian attitudes to others is God's work within us and we can only prevent it. The treatment of others is a problem and a potentiality to which leaders must give serious attention. It is always valuable for a leader to ask himself or herself what is the goal of leadership. This self-questioning should not refer to the possible immediate goals of meeting objectives, or establishing a competitive edge, or achieving growth, and so on. Rather, leaders should ask themselves why it is important to them to be in a leadership position. Do they like being leaders because of the perks that come with the position—increased salaries, fancy offices, free benefits, company car, etcetera? Many do find these material goods enough to work for. It is only necessary to look at the unbalanced benefit packages that some executives seek that do next to nothing except satisfy greed.

Other leaders do not merely long for the material benefits of leadership but rather the sense of respect and *power they feel from having more than others do*, achieving greater successes than others, being in charge of larger organizations than others have. These people have enough goods from their leadership, and what they want now is prestige, respect, power, control, and recognition. Leadership rewards come to these people not from the opportunities to get their hands on more and more material satisfactions, but rather from comparing themselves to others and seeing they are better!

These two approaches to leadership—both of which are very common today—are very selfish and evidence no interest in people unless they can be used to achieve greater material well-being or increased recognition. These are superficial and immature approaches to leadership. Many men and women in positions of potential leadership are too self-centered. They do not care about other people except as means to attain their own goals. However, *successful leadership requires an ability to capitalize on other people's contributions* to an organization. Leadership must include self-training to emphasize the movement away from self-centeredness to self-transcendence with the goal of stressing the central importance of others.

Spiritual leaders appreciate that while achieving the goals of the organization, it is also their task to *respond to other people's deepest needs*, hopes, and dreams. They focus not on their own goals but others' goals and community goals because they believe in people. After all, the leadership problems of recent years have arisen because men and women who could have been leaders instead gave constant priority to themselves rather than to other people. Leaders who give themselves to topics we have reflected on in previous chapters feel their leadership is much more than an opportunity to achieve selfish goals. Leadership must make a difference to other people's lives.

2. Lead with graciousness

How leaders treat other people, especially their co-workers and colleagues, can be a beautiful thing. Of course it can be simply an acquired skill, but it is better when this is the result of deep convictions about other people. *Leaders must ensure that others have a life in keeping with their dignity.* Good leaders will not want followers to be like them, but to be themselves. Such leaders will nurture respect for others in caring leadership and be always grateful to all who work with them and for them. Organizational goals are best achieved by communities in which each member feels valued. Workers perform better when they are trusted, admired, and feel good about themselves. Thus, a spiritual leader must learn how to work with other people so that they feel appreciated.

Leaders need to be aware that they attain their goals with and through others; that *they are incomplete without the gifts of others*. This means giving time to others, getting to know them, and being truly present to them. A leader can show followers that he or she cherishes their presence and talents by giving them opportunities to utilize their gifts, delegating responsible work to them, collaborating, sharing mission values, practicing subsidiarity, and empowering them. A leader who has reflected profoundly on his or her relationship to others always tries to pay attention to the needs of others and to take the risk of being involved with others. This will require a climate of trust that encourages two-way communication, as well as genuine, authentic sharing that allows others to feel safe and comfortable working with their leader. Being a servant leader requires a delicate balance between disturbing the over comfortable and challenging them, along with a willingness at other times to comfort the disturbed. Many times a leader needs to be what others need him or her to be.

Working with others as a leader *starts with graciousness* that includes kindness, warm courtesy, benevolence, and politeness. This means having the grace to show interest in others, being gentle in dealing with them, and letting them know you care. These qualities and gestures come from within a leader and will require humility, patience, and fairness. Such a leader will need empathy and compassion, will care about other people's values, and will have the courage to challenge them. A leader who values people above all else gives them truthful information, values their time and never takes it for granted, and is sensitive to the feelings of others. This is the kind of leader who can become a mentor, can empower others, and can expand and enhance their contributions to shared goals and vision. This leader can persuade others to go the extra mile and find they are glad to be challenged.

It is also part of leadership to become *skillful at celebrating people's successes*, honoring their achievements both informally and formally. A leader should always know what workers have done that merits a word or gesture of recognition. It might be just stopping someone in the corridor to share a compliment and to let them know the leader appreciates what he or she has done. It could be a more formal gathering—although never perfunctory—to celebrate successes. In each case it is a way of giving others visibility. Celebrations are a way of conveying gratitude, affirmation, shared joy, and further anticipated successes. Celebrations also reinforce the organization's values, serve as motivation for others to strive for success, and nurture people's gifts. Learning to rejoice in other people and their gifts is an important quality for leadership. Of course, it is a wonderful part of family life and daily friendship too.

When a person learns how to rejoice in other people and their successes, there follows a series of *positive consequences both for the leader and for followers* too. First, by appreciating the gifts of others one is also preparing oneself for a sense of humility, when one discovers how important other people are. Second, this brings a new perspective to one's leadership, realizing all are important in a common enterprise. Third, celebrating others' contributions generates confidence and therefore hope of more involvement in the future. Fourth, this work produces a sense of common ownership of the mission of the organization. Fifth, in preparing oneself to constantly appreciate the gifts of others a leader is also building up a sense of community. Sixth, if a leader dedicates himself or herself to genuinely create this environment of mutual appreciation then indirectly he or she will control the negativity that frequently inflicts a community of workers.

Perhaps the most important effect of appreciating others and their common efforts for the good of the community is that *a leader begins to sense the value of love* as a major component of leadership. Celebrating others' successes is a way of encouraging the heart of others and cultivating initial aspects of the role of love in leadership.

3. Change focus from self to others

Changing focus from self to others *begins with simple everyday practices*, deliberately appreciating some positive quality of someone else, and taking no one for granted. This includes listening carefully to others when they speak and listening also to their non-verbal communications. It means giving credit to others whenever possible, showing appreciation and gratitude for something they do, recognizing their personal gifts and achievements. This preparation must foster respect for others, a sense of mutuality, and even reverence for other people. It means giving people visibility and prominence.

A spiritual leader *shows others how important they are* to the organization by healing any potential problems in the working environment, by clarifying and refocusing roles so that there is no misunderstanding, by setting goals together so that everyone feels a part, by examining channels of communication so that everyone is kept informed, and by establishing means of recognition. Each person who works for a spiritual leader must feel he or she is handpicked. Spiritual leaders will pay attention to each one, listen carefully to their input, be attentive to them. Leaders let others know they are needed, acknowledge their talents and achievements, and never steal recognition due to them.

Furthermore, focusing on others means *valuing others*, delegating authority to them, encouraging them to participate in decision-making, getting out of their way when they accept responsibility, and celebrating their successes. So, this means removing any injustices that afflict others and then cherishing others and their gifts, even drawing out others' gifts and nurturing their creativity. This implies learning how to make a difference to other people's lives and committing oneself to live and work for community growth.

Part of the responsibility of working with followers is to learn how to *channel their gifts*. The leader must release followers' potential and become a clearing house for their gifts—identifying, channeling, and capitalizing on each one's contribution. Important ways of channeling others' gifts is through delegation and through collaboration when the leader treats followers as partners in a common undertaking. A spiritual leader knows he or she can achieve much more by utilizing others' gifts than by leading on his or her own.

A spiritual leader always wants to have a positive impact on followers and seeks to be *supportive of them in any way possible*. Some will feel supported by a smile, forms of respect, a gesture of kindness, signs of friendship. A spiritual leader must evidence genuine benevolence to followers, thinking well of them even before they ever do anything. The leader stresses good communication, approachability, openness, and understanding. Followers need to know a leader respects them, appreciates them, and likes them—all these responses contribute to an awareness of personal support.

A further way of supporting followers is to *create a pleasant working environment*. The physical environment should be also conducive to workers' calm, peaceful creativity.

A leader's commitment will include speaking with courtesy and pleasantness, sharing significant information, promoting open dialogue, and giving full attention to their questions. Respecting their rights, competencies, levels of authority, duties, and achievements is also a responsibility. By affirming others, fostering a spirit of solidarity, and raising followers' dignity by asking them for help and seeking their feedback on important projects a leader demonstrates the quality of his or her leadership. When a leader can integrate a supportive approach to work with a supportive commitment to personal spiritual development, followers find a deeper meaning in life, and what they learn at work influences the whole of their lives.

A leader knows that without trust there is no likelihood of growth in community spirit or commitment to a shared mission. A spiritual leader *creates a working environment of mutual trust* in which people, relying on the integrity and authenticity of others, always have confident expectations that they will act according to their own values and truth. Trust becomes the emotional glue that binds people together and lets them act as if information is reliable, as if people are competent and motivated, even without solid evidence. When trust is present in an organization, collaboration and partnership are possible; people are free to become their best selves.

A good leader knows how to *confront with compassion*. Followers contribute so much to the community but at times also fail or fall short of expectations at work. A spiritual leader knows that some failure without reprimand is good, and not all failures need to be pointed out to workers or always criticized. Workers often see their own mistakes, evaluate them, and correct them, without any input from management. If a leader needs to criticize the failings of a follower, he or she should do so, generally in private, with compassion, and constructively, so that failure becomes a learning experience and an occasion to strengthen relationships and mutual respect.

Spiritual leaders are not satisfied with providing followers with information, skills, improvement, and attitudinal development—they certainly do all this, but they want to *move their co-workers to personal transformation*. Thus, followers develop a different approach to what they do, to what they see themselves achieving in life. Transformation implies a better way of living and means a person can see beyond the task. The individual is caught up in a mission and vision beyond daily work, becomes a participant in serving the common good and collaborates in influencing the world with values of a vision of hope for humanity.

A leader *guarantees freedom to co-workers*, freedom to be themselves and to express their opinions on issues of importance to the organization. The leader needs to remove any fear in the community, so that workers feel free to express their criticism and even challenge the leader's own approaches to issues. Then, through delegation and collaboration the leader gives followers authority to make their own decisions. However, this freedom is not something that just happens. Rather, it is part of community building that a leader facilitates. Educating people to freedom takes time and effort. A spiritual leader enables freedom among co-workers as part of community building.

When a leader has coached followers well, then he or she must give greater freedom and responsibility to them. The leader must stop making all the decisions, provide adequate information, and then give greater discretion to followers. This means *getting out of their way and letting them feel in charge*. This also implies removing unnecessary rules and regulations that put controls on others' initiative, and restraining oneself from constantly involving oneself in what followers can do well on their own. A spiritual leader accepts subsidiarity as a common practice—letting decisions be made at the lowest level at which they can appropriately be made. This kind of freedom creates responsibility among co-workers. Then, there comes a time when the leader must selflessly let go of followers who have become good leaders.

Valuing people with whom one works is not just a more efficient way of working in organizations but a way of being a more authentic leader. This section of the book is not intended as a practical guide to what a leader can or should do in working collaboratively with others, but as an opportunity to meditate on who we are as human beings. It is intended to challenge anyone who wishes to be a great leader to appreciate that everyone is only a part of our human community, incomplete on one's own, needing the complementarity of others to become our complete selves.

Points for reflection and meditation

- *Describe some of the ways that you neglect other people who work with you or for you.*
- *Do people like to work for you? Why or why not?*
- *What have you learned about how to treat other people?*
- *Specify the ways in which you focus on yourself and the ways you focus on others.*

- *Think about those men and women who have worked for you and who have grown as people because they worked for you.*

CHAPTER EIGHT

LEAD WITH LOVE

"Because of the increase of evil, the love of most will grow cold" (Matthew's Gospel 24:12)

We live in times when many seem to have lost a sense of love and community, while others have discovered the potential impact of values of heart and love. Many leaders have re-appreciated the transforming value of love in organizations. Understanding the importance of love in renewing leadership comes with the other qualities we have seen in previous chapters. It is not a technique; it is a call, a vocation. If leaders fail to respond to this call in their hearts, it will rob them of happiness. This love cannot co-exist with selfishness, and once discovered a leader can never be content with anything less, for the human heart seeks meaning and fulfillment and finds them in love. Leading with love opens up an inner world that touches horizons of life beyond this one. Dedicating oneself to leading with love is a pilgrimage we undertake to find fulfillment, to find our true selves, to find the love for which we were created. Leadership is a matter of heart,[6] and followers quickly perceive whether it is present or not. When they recognize it they become more intimately linked to the leader and the organization, finding a sense of ownership and shared spirit.

Leading with love is a risky undertaking, but leaders must seek never to give up the pursuit of love. The development of love is only possible in a heart that is free from selfishness. One's capacity to lead with love depends on the integrated focus of every aspect of one's life; it cannot be haphazard or episodic but must permeate everything one does. Those who lack love become hard-hearted and their hard-heartedness grows harder and harder, as we have seen in many political and business leaders. Those who lead with love see how wonderful it is to appreciate how the ordinary can be overwhelmed with love.

1. Be magnanimous

Magnanimous" is a little-used word today especially for leaders. It *refers to someone who has a big soul, or a big spirit, or a big heart.* It is a wonderful word to describe a person who longs to deepen his or her calling as a spiritual leader. Such a person has freed himself or herself from inherited prejudice and embodies humaneness, sees whatever good there is in others, and feels enriched by other cultures. This kind of leader has a refined sense of human community. Such a person opens his or her mind to think well of others, appreciates others' views, and probes others to discover their goodness. Such leaders are generally vulnerable, being ever ready to allow others to probe their sense of identity as they do to others.

They are convinced of the mutual enrichment that comes with opening one's heart to welcome everyone. Magnanimity is a quality of great leaders.

Leaders who are magnanimous give themselves generously to others and also gratefully receive from others their self-gift. This *new consciousness concerning mutual enrichment* begins with awareness of the human and global community and how we grow together. Following this awareness comes a desire for greater understanding of other people with whom one works, and an opening of one's mind to know someone better. When done honestly, this leads to fairness and to respect for others' views, whether or not a leader agrees with them.

A leader with these qualities engages in *genuine dialogue with others in the pursuit of truth*. Trust grows when everyone's opinion is considered important. Growth in awareness, understanding, and respect moves a person to acceptance. Even when leaders find that they cannot accept others' views, they certainly accept such people in their own honesty and integrity, and leaders willingly seek means for resolving disputes in a humanly worthy manner. In other words, leaders appreciate others more profoundly than ever, and this appreciation challenges them to value other people and their contributions. These components of magnanimity eventually help leaders to assimilate the goodness of others into a greater consciousness of community.

Part of being magnanimous is to *examine and redirect our attitudes towards others*. We need to correct mistaken attitudes, and free ourselves from unwillingness to collaborate so that we can retain control over vision. These include very negative but common practices of contemporary society that we witness in our daily news; vilifying others and their views, categorizing them without knowing them, giving them labels with artificial, assigned meanings, and perpetuating stereotypes and false assumptions. Spiritual leaders also carefully identify causes of differences and difficulties, otherwise they too easily think of people as victims and perpetrators. Differences often come with social and economic conditioning. Moreover, spiritual leaders appreciate that differences are not necessarily blocks to healthy communication and mutual appreciation; in fact, they can enhance these dimensions of lives. Above all, such leaders always presume everyone who is at least moderately mature wants positive relationships.

Leaders who wish to be magnanimous will strategize to become so. This includes resisting all judgmental attitudes towards others—a difficult task in our contemporary society, known for its constant mutual blame. Then, they must learn to excel in listening skills, seeking feedback from others to help check how they perceive others, and then refocusing. These people also cultivate a new self-awareness that includes others as integral to a vision of themselves.

There is no way to avoid taking risks in deepening relationships with others. In fact, risk taking is integral to the strategy of a magnanimous person. Finally, the goal of each of these strategies is always the same—to *let others find a place in a leader's heart,* even those with whom he or she disagrees. Being magnanimous contributes so positively to opening minds that can then be enriched by new ideas.

At the same time good leaders are not naïve nor are they fools. There is an increasing number of individuals and groups who are totally given to intolerance. They earn money—lots of it, and gain supporters exclusively because they are obsessed with bigotry and intolerance. *Without mutuality and openness there can be no genuine dialogue.* Spiritually dedicated individuals must struggle when results are possible but should not waste time.

2. Show tolerance and compassion

We live in a world that is increasingly intolerant, one in which violence, untruthfulness, hate, mutual criticism abound, and people constantly and deliberately do hurtful things to others. Our culture is one of opposition, confrontation, rejection, polarization, and widespread intolerance. People are paid lots of money to be intolerant, and they gather around them a large following of insecure individuals who delight to find their own intolerant attitudes supported by celebrities in the media, or politics or religion. These political, social, and religious "leaders" whip their followers into a frenzy over issues that are not central to their original vision, leading to catastrophes like ethnic cleansing, or even to the deliberate, destructive intention of labeling others to demean or destroy them. People develop skills that foster intolerance, challenging spiritual leaders to be equally skilled in opposing it.

Intolerant individuals are generally uninformed or ignorant, either by force of circumstances or by a deliberate closed mindedness—a desire not to learn what other people think or feel. Their deafness to others' views and their unwillingness to search for common ground give rise to a hatred for anyone who thinks differently than themselves.

Closed mindedness atrophies thought, but since knowledge is the basis of love it also stunts any ability to grow in understanding and love. Closed mindedness is not a normal characteristic of human beings who innately search for meaning, understanding, and enlightenment. But, people are trained and initiated into closed mindedness generally by social, political, educational, or religious figures. Some local groups or entire nations are known for their open-mindedness and others for their closed mindedness. However, intolerant behavior is now a serious cultural problem and a major challenge for leaders in all walks of life.

Most people do not think they are intolerant. Rather, they have *false justification for their behavior*. Many think they are being principled, consider their views the only acceptable ones, and see any attempt to understand others as weakness. Our society is riddled with extreme fundamentalism in politics, choice of political parties, judicial practice, approaches to foreign policy, and all sorts of issues in social and religious life. Litmus tests are everywhere, and any divergence from the acceptable, myopic views is rejected, and those who hold different views are despised. Some of the most complicated contemporary issues receive simplistic answers from people who will not or cannot think things through. Such people often act like bulldozers, flattening all other ideas in their path.

Leaders who seek spiritual depth need to reject all forms of intolerant behavior. This will mean first and foremost accepting the need to constantly learn anew, to appreciate that some change and adaptability guarantees the genuineness of values we hold. *Never to change means always to live in the past.* Leaders must have exceptional listening skills to understand others' words, their deeper yearnings, their struggles, and their hopes. They will need to be people of genuine dialogue, even with others who lack such skills. Such leaders can read and study with the desire to be more informed. From time to time they should rethink their own views, either to conclude in reaffirming them or to change them when they notice a loss of focus. So many drag along behind them ideas from the past, emphasize what dedication and discipleship used to be two thousand years ago, and end up worshipping a god from their high school years or a god of their own creation. Intolerant behavior that closes the door on new ways of thinking and doing leads to myopic approaches that quickly destroy society—civic and religious.

One of the *best responses to intolerance is compassion*. Compassion is one of the most beautiful qualities that we can extend to others. If leaders train themselves to make this an intentional response, they draw out an energy of the spirit that can transform society. Compassion means "to suffer with," and it describes being with others in the intimacy of their pain. Compassion means feeling the way others do in their suffering, enduring the pain with them, and supporting them in mutual efforts. Compassion is a healing service to others, journeying with them through the difficulties of their lives. When one experiences compassion it transforms one's inner life and leads one to be compassionate towards others.

Our contemporary world is no different than it has been in other times; it gives *little evidence of compassion*. Rather, it is often characterized by selfishness, greed, and abuse of others. So many seem to choose dominant, hateful approaches to others. When we show compassion, the evil of this world cannot deal with it. They certainly cannot oppose it for it is clearly a genuine quality, at the heart of humanity. In fact, evil people in our world do not know what to do with compassion. They see it, silently appreciate it, sometimes mock it as weakness, but can never oppose it.

Leaders should show compassion to themselves and their own failures, to others in their many needs, to the world when the environment is abused. There is so much pain, loss, sickness, and abuse. People are marginalized and discriminated against for all kinds of reasons. A leader's compassion needs to be practical and implies fighting for justice; *it has to be more than a believed-in compassion*, it has to be real. This will imply not being afraid to show feelings and emotions as leaders suffer together with those in pain. Such leaders also need to identify the causes of pain, to seek alleviation in the short term where possible, and to pursue solutions for situations that bring so much torment and suffering. Sometimes there are no solutions to the pain people feel. It might be a terminal illness that has no end except further pain and death. It could be the loss of loved ones, tragically taken in war or in a natural disaster. Often for coworkers there is really nothing we can do. We all need to be together in mutual compassion faced with a mystery we do not understand. We strive to be together, to console each other, to sustain each other's commitment, and to let each other know our love.

3. Transform values with love

Consumerism has corrupted our world and even our spirituality. We always want more of everything—whether objects, experiences, position, people's praise, and so on. We have so many objects that we claim to love and need. For those readers who are Christians it is important to remember that in his life and teachings *the first priority Jesus gives us is to love God and one's neighbor above all el*se. We cannot disperse the power of our love among endless secondary objects. Rather, leaders who are believers focus the full strength of their love on God and on their neighbors as signs of God's presence among us. Much of what we want and claim to love can only be ours at other people's expense. Comparing ourselves to others—their position, salary, the praise they receive, their promotions, and so on, always leads us away from love.

Striving to lead with love is a long journey in which love matures gradually. Love is shown day by day in small steps, and an important part of every day is that we *make decisions based always on what is the most loving thing to do*. This takes time, self-training, and discernment. It means evaluating every decision we need to make and seeing the pros and cons of each one, asking ourselves which decisions would lead to harm and which would lead to good, harmony, and love. At first, this will take a lot of time but with practice it becomes almost spontaneous. In fact, when love is present in any organization it becomes redemptive and transformative for all in the organization. However, it is through our decisions that we manifest our values and priorities. Consequently this is a practice worth fostering.

Love starts in community and is part of all our efforts to *build unity and community* today. Community requires real and reciprocal relationships and members build up strong communities with simple expressions of humanity, care, trust, and support. It also needs creative tolerance of differences, solidarity, and peacemaking. All groups have their own stages in psychological development and members will need to respect these different stages, and Christians will need to channel the group through its positive and painful growth stages. Love-based leadership capitalizes on our differences, builds solidarity, and creates commitment to a common vision.

Maintaining the priority of *love requires constant evaluation*. This vision of love is important, a matter of life and death. Jesus calls disciples to decide what kind of people they want to become. Will we build our lives on the love that Jesus taught or will we give ourselves to non-love? There is nothing in-between. This is the most essential decision of life. Love is the norm for judging Christian character. The world, each of us, can respond to the challenge of love or choose a world of selfishness and hatred.

We cannot merely believe in the power of love, we must act on that conviction and *show our dedication in action*. This means making decisions based on the most loving thing to do. When we live in this way, we ourselves are the first focus of transformation. We change our own attitudes to life, rejecting selfishness, greed, and self-satisfaction, and thus we move away from self-centeredness to self-transcendence. This is a rigorous self-training and eventually leads to the integration of all aspects of life in loving self-gift to others. This single-hearted pursuit of the way of love transforms our decisions, actions, and purposes in life.

When we are motivated by our conviction of the transforming value of love, we treat others with a natural benevolence. We wish them well before any encounter, appreciate the good in others, and presume that they will do good. This *positive, optimistic approach to others* has a healing effect on relationships and opens up the development of friendships that are mutually enriching. The development of love-based friendships prepares us for our journey of love and the fostering of deeper relationships with other people in community and with God.

Leaders who believe in the power of love can approach the development even of their own family life in a new enriched way. *Family provides the basic encounter of love* and is ideally also a school of love where all members can learn from each other and reach out beyond the boundaries of family life to spread their treasure of love to others. The family group is a community of love wherein human qualities mature. Husband, wife, and children, in total solidarity, enrich one another and together bring into being human values otherwise unattainable. These values then extend to every aspect of leadership.

There is an intimate connection between our individual growth in love and our growth as communities of love. Unfortunately, we do not always see loving communities, and the contemporary challenge for those who believe in the power of love is to foster reconciliation. St. Paul summed up the whole thrust of Jesus' ministry as the work of reconciliation and saw his own ministry as one of reconciliation (2 Cor 5:18-19). Our world today desperately needs a spirit of ongoing reconciliation in friendships, families, political discussion, national vision, and international endeavors. As Christians, working for reconciliation is an essential dimension of our call in faith to love others. This includes repentance, a change of mentality, and mutual forgiveness. It also means reaching out to the marginalized or rejected, respecting others' opinions, and building bridges. *Bringing others together in reconciliation* strengthens our common dedication to pursue the way of love.

When we understand the transforming power of love, it becomes the source of our energy to change unacceptable realities. Each of us needs to develop our own personal philosophy of leadership. We often live with an illusion that our leadership is the best it can be when it would be transformed by love in to something totally different.

Points for reflection and meditation

- What place does love have in your leadership?
- Do you learn a lot from people who work for you? Give examples.
- In what ways are you tolerant and in what ways are you intolerant?
- In a world that lacks compassion do others who know you see you as an exception?
- How is reconciliation a part of your life and leadership?

ENDNOTES

1. For further reflections on leisure, see my book *Leisure: A Spiritual Need* (Wipf and Stock, 2017).
2. See Spitzer, Robert J. *The Spirit of Leadership* (Provo, UT: Executive Excellence Pubishing, 2000), chapter 6: "Four Levels of Happiness."
3. This section is based on notes taken from an article, "Orvieto: la capitale della lentezza," in La Repubblica, 12 February 2005, 36-37.
4. See Spitzer, pp. 33-36: "Seven Effects of Spirit."
5. Pope Francis, Christmas message, 2014.
6. Here are just two quotes of many that stress the importance of love. "And what sustains the leader? From what source comes the leader's courage? The answer is love. Leaders are in love—in love with people who do the work, with what their organizations produce, and with their customers." Kouzes, James M., and Posner, Barry Z. *The Leadership Challenge* (San Francisco: Jossey Bass Inc., Publishers, 1987, p. 239). "The heart of leadership is in the hearts of leaders. You have to lead from something deep in your heart." Bolman, Lee G. and Deal, Terrance. *Leading with Soul: An Uncommon Journey of Spirit* (San Francisco: Jossey-Bass Publishers, 1995), p. 21

For more detailed development of material in chapters 3 (77-80) and 5 (46-50) see my book, *Courageous Hope* (New York/Mahwah,NJ: Paulist Press, 2011), chps. 5 and 3.

Readers interested in spiritual leadership can read my blog and contribute a comment

leonarddoohan.wordpress.com

See Leonard Doohan's webpage at
leonarddoohan.com

All books are available on Amazon.com

THREE BOOKS ON SPIRITUAL LEADERSHIP

How to Become a Great Spiritual Leader: Ten Steps and a Hundred Suggestions

This is a book for daily meditation. It has a single focus—how to become a great spiritual leader. It is a book on the spirituality of a leader's personal life. It presumes that leadership is a vocation, and that it results from an inner transformation. The book proposes ten steps that individuals can take to enable this process of transformation, and a hundred suggestions to make this transformation real and lasting. It is a unique book in the literature on leadership.

This book is the third in a series on leadership. The first, *Spiritual Leadership: The Quest for Integrity* gave the foundations of leadership today. The second, *Courageous Hope: The Call of Leadership*, gave the contemporary characteristics and qualities of leadership. This third book focuses on the spirituality of the leader.

Courageous Hope: The Call of Leadership

Paulist Press

This book's focus on leadership and hope is very appropriate given today's climate of distrust that many find results in a sense of hopelessness in their current leaders. Individuals and organizations are desperate for leaders of hope. Many books on leadership point to the need for inner motivation, but that inner motivation must be hope in new possibilities for a changed future. It is hope that gives a meaningful expression to leadership and enables the leader to be creative in dealing with the present. More than anything else it is a vision of hope that can excite and empower leaders to inspire others to strive for a common vision.

"Doohan strengthens our resolve. He restores our hope. And in an echo of Robert Frost, he is not only a teacher, but an awakener. May this book find you in a place where your will to grow is matched by an inner radiance to serve and help heal those around you… the reading will meet you there and the end result will be a gift to the world." **Shann Ray Ferch, PhD, MFA** Professor and Chair, Doctoral Program in Leadership Studies, Gonzaga University. Editor, International Journal of Servant Leadership.

"Read every word of this book. Leaders stuck in the past, afraid to face the future, afraid to take a risk because they might be wrong need an infusion of *Courageous Hope*. People are not looking for a simple, blind-faith hope. They are looking for leaders with a deeper understanding of hope as described in this book. **Mary McFarland, PhD** Professor, and Former Dean of undergraduate through doctoral programs in Leadership. International consultant in leadership and education.

"Ask people who were alive during the Great Depression what a huge difference Franklin Roosevelt made in their lives by giving them reasons to be hopeful. Ask people who were alive during the papacy of John XXIII what they loved most about him, and chances are they'll say that "good Pope John" gave them hope for the future. Read *Courageous Hope* and learn how to be that kind of leader yourself." **Mitch Finley,** Author of over 30 award winning books.

Spiritual Leadership: The Quest for Integrity

Paulist Press

In eight clear and challenging chapters, the reader is invited to partake of a rich menu of reflections on the meaning of spiritual leadership and how it can transform one's role in the workplace, ensuring a collaborative environment of trust and confidence that energizes not only the culture of an organization, but also the effective accomplishment of its mission.

Leonard Doohan's highly readable book presents leadership as a call motivated by faith and love that results in a change of life, a conversion, and a breakthrough to a new vision of one's role in the world.

"Leonard Doohan's *Spiritual Leadership* is a profound and caring work . . . I highly recommend it to anyone interested in the spiritual meaning of servant leadership." **Larry C. Spears.**

"'The leader within,' . . . is well served by Leonard Doohan's book, *Spiritual Leadership*. It is a profound guidebook for leaders of the future, who live their values, who keep the faith. **Frances Hesselbein.** Chair, Leader to Leader Institute

Dr. Leonard Doohan's new volume on *Spiritual Leadership* reaches beyond, or perhaps better, beneath the many current volumes on leadership which emphasize skill sets, techniques, and learned habits." **Robert J. Spitzer, SJ, PhD.** President and CEO, Magis Institute

Another book of interest

Enjoying Retirement: Living Life to the Fullest

Paulist Press

A book for leaders in retirement. This book is for a new kind of retiree—including the baby-boomer generation—who seeks to deal with retirement years not as an end of usefulness but as a major period in life with its own challenges that need practical responses and depth of understanding. Christian spirituality refers to the way we live our daily lives in the challenge of faith. Clearly, the years of retirement offer the most important occasion for each of us to respond to this challenge of making a new beginning.

This wise and engaging book offers wonderful opportunities to discover how to approach retirement—now as much as a third of life for many—with enthusiasm, anticipation, creativity, and enjoyment as the best and blessed time of our lives.

All books are available from amazon.com